WITHDRAWN

PARADOX

A Round Trip Through the Bermuda Triangle

by
Nicholas R. Nelson

DORRANCE & COMPANY • *Ardmore, Pennsylvania*

Contents

Preface

PARADOX—A statement that is seemingly contradictory and yet is true.

CALL ME A NON-EXPERT, for I bring no particular academic degrees into the arena with me and, therefore, claim the right to be wrong. But I also claim the right to be right, and my credit cards in life's game are a voracious reading appetite, undying curiosity, and the ability to ask questions, some of which are so strange they may not have been asked before.

I went through a long period of self-criticism before starting this task because, frankly, the conclusions at which I finally arrived were a little weird, but my questioning could not shake the conclusions, so, like an amateur flasher, I expose myself, if not timidly, then with certain reservations. I'm new at this sort of thing and, perhaps, worried about remarks concerning my shortcomings. But, as can be seen, I've overcome the shyness and set my ideas loose on the public.

If my efforts do not enlighten I hope they will at least entertain. There will be some, however, who, when this small book falls into their hands, will get angry, and to them I can only relate a suspicion which jolts me awake from time to time. The longer I remain alive in this topsy-turvy world of ours, the more certain I become that this business of living is taken entirely too seriously.

v

Introduction

THE BERMUDA TRIANGLE phenomenon and the mysteries which have made this area infamous have long been a subject of literary investigation. Through movies, television specials, and many books and articles the public has been drowned in facts, figures, and umpteen ideas designed to popularize the mystery. The whole thing and its attendant craziness has been done, undone, and redone by anyone who thinks he has a new angle or spectacular incident to report. So, were it not for the gentle insistence of friends, I would not have sought to add my voice to the clamor. Even beyond these friendly nudgings I would have kept my observations private had it not been for a strange, rather ludicrous conversation between myself and a good friend while driving home from a vacation.

The conversation, though not directly concerning the Bermuda Triangle, grandly illustrates the horrendous problem involved in speaking about the unspeakable and discussing that which cannot be properly discussed.

We were somewhere in southern Oregon, angling northwest, in clear, sunny April weather, returning from a weekend jaunt to Winnemucca, Nevada. My friend was driving toward a distant, ominous storm front while I was enjoying being a passenger and reading an April fool's article in a magazine devoted to science and science fiction. The article was written with tongue in cheek, taking a quasi-serious stance about a conclusion to a subject almost anyone with a dime's worth of intelligence would regard as silly.

As the author of the article no doubt intended, at first I thought he was serious when he began discussing a point of view regarding gravity. Somewhere in the middle of the piece, however, I realized I was being put on, and in this vein I enjoyed the article so much I read it to my friend as he drove through the monotonous countryside. Both of us had a good laugh, but something was nagging at me. As foolish as the article was, if I paused just long enough to turn off my working knowledge of the world, it almost made sense. For instance, the author made the bald-faced claim that a jet plane does not stay up at extremely high altitudes because of the lift of air rushing over scientifically designed wings. Well, stop and think about that. There is almost no air at the altitudes at which many jets fly. The author was joking, of course, but if a plane stays up because of lift, and there is little or no air to provide lift, what happens to the commonly accepted theory of flight? The author claimed a jet stays up because, as it is moved under power, its accumulated mass gathers up what he referred to as "staticons." Staticons, explained the article, are particles of "static gravity" acquired by laterally moving objects. In other words, a kind of strange form of antigravity.

I didn't keep the real world shut off for long, though, and I left that nagging feeling behind, laughing at this silly premise just as the author had intended. About the time we had extracted most of the fun from the article, my friend rolled down the driver's side window and threw out a big wad of chewing gum which had lost its flavor. But the gum uncooperatively flew back in the car, ending up in the middle of the back seat. Still chuckling, I reached back to retrieve it and while involved in this saw another chance to milk more mirth out of the nutty concept of staticons.

"Now look at this, John," I said seriously, exhibiting the sticky gum wad. "This gum couldn't leave the car because it had too big a charge of staticons."

Wondering if I had left my mind back on one of Winnemucca's twenty-one tables along with my money, he asked, "Now how do you figure that?"

"Simple," I replied, getting a feel for the argument. "Here we are traveling down the road at fifty-five miles per hour. You and I are moving at the same speed with the car, and so is the gum. So when you tried to throw it out the window it was still traveling forward at fifty-five, and because you did not toss it with enough lateral force to counteract its stored up forward moving staticons, the gum had no choice but to rejoin us."

Sputtering, he pointed out that the wind had simply blown the gum back in. Now really into the spirit of the charade, I asked him, "What wind?"

He waved his hand to cover the outdoors beyond the windshield. "There's a fifty-five mile per hour wind out there."

"There's no wind out there, John," I pointed out. "Look at the grass and sagebrush. The air's dead still."

"No, no," he protested. "The car's making the wind I'm talking about."

"I'll grant you," I agreed, "that this car is stirring up the air as it passes through, but I don't think it's fair to call it a wind. After all, when we're half a mile down the road no wind will be blowing at this spot."

"Well, anyway," he said, ignoring this bit of twisted logic, "that 'stirred up air' is what blew the gum back in."

Having started this bit of merriment I couldn't leave it. So to further confuse the issue I related to my companion a childhood experience when I had noticed a fly buzzing around inside my parents' car. Being very young and, therefore, honestly ignorant, I asked the big people in the front seat why the fly was not plastered against the rear window instead of flying freely around the interior. To my poor young mind the fly had no business being at rest in midair inside a vehicle moving at fifty miles per hour. I was told by the big people that the windshield allowed the fly to do its impossible act. Since the air inside the car was moving with the car, so, too, must the fly move with the air, moving with the car.

I accepted that explanation as factual, but at that tender age had my parents rendered an account of static gravity generating staticons through the action of a moving vehicle making the fly relative to the interior of the car, I probably would have accepted that as well. As a matter of fact, such an explanation would have fitted right in with the observation which prompted the question.

"So you see, John," I told my driver, "because of staticons building up because of our velocity, you and I and this wad of gum are at rest relative to the car which is not at rest relative to the ground. When you tossed the gum out the window it was still at rest relative to the car. Simple."

He coughed at this bit of dubious wisdom, perhaps wishing he was not out in the middle of nowhere with a man suddenly gone crazy.

Noting his continuing skepticism I said, "I'll prove it to you." And holding the wad of gum out over the floor I dropped it between my legs. "There you have it. The gum fell from my hand straight down to the floorboard. Just like the fly, the gum is relative to the moving car. Staticons!"

"Now just a damn minute," countered my befuddled friend, hoping he had a handle on me at last. "What would that look like to someone standing outside as we passed by?"

I leaped gleefully on to that one. "From the outside, stationary point of reference the gum would have seemed to go forward from the point where it was dropped to the point where it landed. Why do you think that's so?"

"Because of inertia," he answered, and then proceeded to give me a short course in basic physics. "The gum is traveling fifty-five miles per hour, and when you let go of it, it tended to keep going in the direction of travel, but the car, also going fifty-five, moved under it, so it looked to us like it fell in a straight line, but to someone outside it would have looked as though it went forward for a bit."

I had him trapped. I pointed out that if inertia had anything to do with my demonstration, then the gum once out of my fingers would no longer be under power and would have had to slow down relative to the constant speed of the automobile. If inertia was operating then the gum would have had to seem to make a rearward move from our point of view. I was destroying his every counterclaim by simply switching my argument to another point of reference. I had sucked him through the looking glass, and for the next half hour or so, using the oddball concept of staticons, Newton's laws, and the theory of relativity, I had poor John ready to check into a universe less complicated and weird than this one.

At one point I held the gum out the window at arm's length, dramatically dropped it, and proceeded to develop separate arguments as to what happened to the gum:

A. Since the gum was at rest when I let it go it fell straight down. (The wind must be discounted, of course.)
B. Since the gum was traveling at fifty-five miles per hour it tended to travel ahead, slowing down because it was no longer under power. (Also forgetting the wind.)
C. The gum took off almost horizontally from my hand at fifty-five miles per hour backwards, forming a sensible trajectory from my hand before hitting the ground behind us. (Proof of this could come from someone in the back seat with his hand out the window to catch the gum wad fired at fifty-five miles per hour from my hand.)

About the time the subject of the artificial wind came up for the umpteenth time fun was fading from the debate, and John would not even let me expound on what happened strictly from the gum's point of view.

We finally agreed, though, on why my childhood fly managed to buzz around inside my parents' car. After the hilarity of our conversation the solution was completely and totally obvious. The fly, we agreed, could do what it did because nobody had ever told it that it could not do what it did.

Likewise, we agreed, the law of gravity is not an immutable law at all, but simply a way of talking about things which fall down.

As acknowledged, none of the above conversation has anything directly to do with the Bermuda Triangle, but it was the magazine article, and the friendly argument fostered by it, which finally spurred me to put into print what I think I know about the subject. In discussing the Bermuda Triangle phenomenon with friends I generally end by convincing most of them of my conclusions, but whenever I have considered revealing to the world this "truth" of mine I have balked because I realize my truth is no more than theory. Not a truth at all, but, hopefully, an understandable, self-evident truism.

Also, I don't really care to take on the orthodox scientific community which will tend to snicker as I snickered at the magazine article about static gravity. I also put myself in the shoes of my relatives who would be asked if they were related to that nut who thinks he has solved the riddle of the universe by expounding on the myth of the Bermuda Triangle. Well, I suppose the snickering will come, and it will come because in talking about this subject I will be forced to deal with simplistic explanations. It will come because I will be forced to use words normally used for other things and events and forced to do so because no words have yet been invented to cover the things and events about which I will talk.

It may seem to a scientist that I am violating the concept of physicalism, which is a thesis that the descriptive terms of scientific language are reducible to terms which refer to space, temporal things, or events. If I am to speak at all there is no way to avoid this kind of confrontation, and I can do nothing at all about another's point of view except to try and show him the view from my side of the fence.

I realize I am defending myself before the fact, and perhaps this is not good editorial policy, but I would like the reader to enter the experience of this book with as open a mind as possible, and I wish for the reader to understand that I will have to invent a new way to talk about things which disappear.

Inventing a new way to talk about something is one of the best ways for a person to get the label of crank pinned to him. If the author of the article about staticons had been serious, perhaps he would be regarded as no more than a harmless crank. But had he put forward this novel idea before the world heard of Newton and gotten enough of his colleagues to agree with him, thus forming the Law of Static Gravity, then Newton would have been judged the crank. If I may paraphrase the master, if he knew what he was doing then he was "blest," but if he did not know what he was doing then he was "truly cursed." I feel, in my own mind at least, that I know what I am doing. I know there are those who will call me a crank. I no longer care. It came to me on that ride through sagebrush and potholes that all points of view are valid. A high flying jet plane may stay up because of wing lift or because of staticons. It doesn't matter really. What matters is that most of us agree that because we can witness the event of the plane staying up the rest is merely another agreement on how we wish to speak about the subject.

Another part of my earlier reluctance to write on this subject has been the ability to see both sides of the argument. For instance, being an inventive sort, there have been times in the past when I have lamented scientific dogma, yet I understand the need for such dogma. Consider the state of science if every scientist went flying off after every inventive idea presented by every crank. Chaos would be the only result because no one would be able to agree on anything. Yet even knowing this, I cannot accept the dogma of black *or* white. I see all problems as black *and* white.

Seeing things this way makes it difficult to take a solid stand, but there is one irrefutable fact which put my fingers to work on the keys, and I offer it to the reader in the hope that it will carry him through.

Paradox is real! Paradox absolutely exists. Both sides of the fence are as real as the fence is real. In this book I can be wrong and still be right. Science can be right and still be wrong.

My personal paradox is taking a stand when I know the stand I'm taking is subject to agreement by those who will probably not agree with me. Many will see my explanations as absurd, but it is a matter of rights rather than wrongs. It is, my indisputable right to appear absurd in the eyes of others, and it is their indisputable right to hold that opinion.

So before I begin in earnest to unfold my theory of the Bermuda Triangle I will, also before the fact, apologize to science and to any scientific people who may read this treatise. Please understand it is not my purpose to try to impose an idea on nature, but, by using familiar terms in my own way and by trying not to invent new symbolism, I'm attempting to explain what I believe I have seen in nature. Indeed, if one is in agreement with me at the end of this book, he will readily recognize that the above sentence contains an unavoidable error because by agreeing with me he will have accepted the notion that no matter what anyone says about nature it is an imposition.

The reader is about to encounter a simplistic explanation about a complicated subject. The subject is complicated because by using familiar words to explain an intangible a reliance on symbolism is necessary. There has not been a previously agreed way of discussing the conclusions drawn from the evidence, and, regardless of whose theory of the Bermuda Triangle finally is accepted, the acceptance will depend entirely on an agreement of the language to be used.

Should I have been able to ask the fly for an explanation of its dramatic flight inside the moving car, I can well imagine its simplistic answer suitable for all flys:

"Idiot. Can't you see I have wings?"

In the viewpoint of this book, versus the generally accepted viewpoint, I am the fly buzzing around inside the moving automobile, and no one told me I cannot do what I am doing.

There is a quote from a 1926 conversation with Albert Einstein that is an appropriate ending for these introductory comments. If one wishes to boil several thousand words down into a few, Dr. Einstein's words sum up the evidentual nature of this book: "It is quite wrong to try founding a theory on observable magnitudes alone. In reality the very opposite happens. It is the theory which decides what we can observe."

I would hope my small efforts might bring about one of those very few revelations in science, but, by knowing what I am doing, I'm not holding my breath.

CHAPTER ONE

Locating the Evidence

THIS WORK IS MAINLY prepared for those who already have some
working knowledge of the infamous area of our globe most often
referred to as the Bermuda Triangle. Therefore this is not a
rehash of old and, by now, familiar incidents, but an
examination of those events already well chronicled by so many
other books and films. Other works on this subject have
provided much empirical evidence and incident by incident
examination of documented events, so we do not have to rely
on blind faith to know this mystery truly exists within some
part of the fabric of what we perceive to be reality.

Earlier works on this topic have been telling the tale of a trail
into the unknown, and it is my hopeful intention to be able to
show the nature of this path and at least one of its useful
directions. But before setting foot on this trail the reader should
be told that an understanding of what lies at the end will
ultimately demand a larger acceptance of reality and a radically
different view of world structure.

Just as those in the time of Copernicus and Galileo resisted
the notion of a round world no longer at the center of the
universe, some of those who pursue the problems inherent in
the Triangle mystery will resist conclusions drawn here. Simply
stated, the reader's world view must change or the concepts
revealed will be rejected, for in order to understand this mystery
and make it commonplace, one must deal with the difficult
mental concept of infinity.

There would be some small but unsettling comfort in this
concept to the sixteenth century accusers of Galileo, for having
once found one's self living in infinity one's place is always at
the center of the universe.

1

We have piles of information from investigating the Bermuda Triangle phenomenon which does not seem to fit into the neat idea of reality most of us believe we live in. We call this a mystery, and perhaps some of us would prefer it remain a mystery or even wish it would go away so as not to trouble an otherwise orderly world. A mystery tantalizes the mind and provides a puzzle to solve, but a puzzle once solved is often cast aside. A solution renders the puzzle into just another piece of world furniture, now known and suddenly commonplace. Like a person trying to fit pieces of a puzzle back into the special shape in which it came, we cry, "Don't tell me the answer. I want to find it myself." But there are others who want help with their puzzle, and that is what this work is trying to give.

The principle of causality demands that an event be preceded by a cause. Myth, it has been noticed, always comes before reality. Many of us are intrigued by the cause of the events reported in the Bermuda Triangle, and we grope and search for the reality which, at the moment, is the myth suggested by the events. This is more than just a mystery. It is an ambiguous enigma. An obscure puzzle sent to us already disassembled, without instructions. And to make matters worse, these equivocal pieces are not all in the box.

I could have made this a much longer book by padding it with graphic accounts of disappearing planes, ships, people, and strange experiences, but this would be mere repetition. The public, for the most part, knows about these things, and it is my opinion that it is time to pull them together to form the larger and, finally, the more comprehensive picture. I will not detail specific events unless the details would add substance to the picture. It is not the events themselves which interest me, but how and why they occur.

Lying off the coast of Florida within lines drawn from Miami to Bermuda, from there to near Puerto Rico, and back to Miami, is the well-known area recognized as the Bermuda Triangle. Here, within and around this imaginary triangle, we have been told of ships, planes, and people disappearing from the very face of the earth with alarming frequency. As if to test our credulity many of these disappearances leave few or no clues as to their ultimate fates.

2

This is a situation regarded as abnormal within the perceptual limits of our real three-dimensional world. For instance, if a plane crashes off the coast of California or if a ship wrecks near Maine, pieces of the wrecks frequently are found which give decipherable clues as to the fates of the people and machines involved. However, when there are no clues at all when there should be something, anything, or when the few clues found are beyond our knowledge of what we normally regard as existent, another kind of reality is suggested, and then, because there is no known criteria by which to judge, resisted.

When a boat struggles into port after a storm, its decks awash, its masts broken, and its hull damaged, we know beyond doubt that wind and sea, acting in predictable violence, caused the damage. This is a consequence of living in the real three-dimensional world, and we all understand the cause of the effects witnessed. But when a plane lands several minutes late after vanishing off a radar scope, with all timepieces aboard inexplicably ten minutes behind those on the ground, we are threatened with the loss of some of our carefully guarded concepts of reality.

Other works on this subject have mystified us, and many have offered solutions. Some surmise that the lost continent of Atlantis lies beneath those waters, and that still functioning machinery, decidedly esoteric in nature, or that even living inhabitants of the sunken civilization, are responsible for the disappearances. Some claim UFOs from other worlds are using the area as a hunting ground for human specimens, and, indeed, an inordinate number of UFOs are seen in this area. Others hypothesize a time or interdimensional warp; cosmic rays; some sort of antigravitation effect tossing selected things into outer space; giant fireballs of ball lightning; or whirlpools, clear air turbulence, sea serpents, tidal waves, waterspouts, earthquakes, seaquakes, general bad weather, modern pirates active in the drug traffic, even a mind over matter psychokinesis effect.

It appears the actual truth cannot lie in any one of the many hypotheses so far offered, but may rest somewhere in between or be regarded as a cause-effect relationship of many of the solutions already proposed. When attempting to unravel the

3

secrets of an unknown factor a theory fitting the facts must be erected from as sound a footing as possible. Since the evidence of the activity in the Bermuda Triangle has only a peripheral relationship to that which is known, the theory must be constructed from everything which is known and accepted, even if such evidence seems outwardly to have nothing to do directly with the mystery. The pieces of this jigsaw puzzle are hidden all around the house, so the theory first must locate the pieces and put them on the table. To be comprehensible the theory must first find the pieces which have been overlooked by others. If the forest is to be seen we must first back away from the trees.

This book looks at such a theory. A theory which incorporates parts of some of the already public hypotheses about the Bermuda Triangle phenomenon with new bits and pieces of information. Hopefully it is a balanced theory, logically constructed, and, given the proper interest, experimentally provable in some cases.

CHAPTER TWO

Assembling the Evidence

THE FIRST PIECE OF information which I fit into the mosaic is the little publicized fact that the Bermuda Triangle is but one of several such areas located about the globe. The second best known Triangle area where strange disappearances take place is popularly known as the Devil's Triangle, or the Devil's Sea, located just east of the East China Sea, and south of Japan. This area in its way is just as infamous as the Bermuda zone, and when one locates both places on a world map a striking coincidence is noticed. Both areas lay between the same lines of latitude, varying between seventeen degrees north latitude, and thirty-three degrees north latitude. This one fact alone does not prove anything special, but a careful perusal of other literature yields knowledge of another area of similar mystery in a little traveled area over Afghanistan. During World War II this area became much traveled by pilots flying supplies into China "over the hump" of the Himalayas. Out of that adventure came the usual stories of disappearing airplanes, fouled up instruments, and even a reported sighting of a giant white pyramid. This area of the world lies near enough to the same northern latitudes as Bermuda and the Devil's Sea to cause more than just a little suspicion.

On a smaller scale similar reports of disappearances come from an area slightly northeast of Hawaii and from another spot located near Morocco. Both of these lesser known spots also rest near the same lines of latitude as the Bermuda Triangle. Thus there are five similar zones in the northern hemisphere of the planet Earth where the known laws of reality are now and then bent out of shape. The most important clue in this observation is that each area is approximately equidistant from the other, about forty-seven hundred miles as the crow flies.

At near equal distances from each other the five Triangle zones located in the northern hemisphere are not alone. There are five more important clues in the southern hemisphere. Off the coast of Chile with Easter Island slightly southwest of its center is another area of strangeness. Proceeding west we find stories of strange disappearances coming from an area north of New Zealand. From west of Australia and south of Indonesia have come more weird reports. Between Madagascar and the southern tip of Africa and in the empty ocean east of Rio de Janeiro comes word of the last two mysterious areas. Interestingly, each of these areas is also on the exact same southern latitudinal lines, between seventeen degrees south latitude and thirty-three degrees south latitude, and, as with their northern counterparts, also nearly exactly the same distance apart from each other. They are forty-seven hundred miles apart, but each southern Triangle area rests on lines of longitude halfway between their northern hemisphere neighbors, and the distance between any southern Triangle to the nearest northern Triangle is about forty-eight hundred miles.

Although most of these spots have received very little publicity each of them is responsible for haunted sea stories of disappearing ships, planes, and people. All but two of these so-called Triangle zones are located over water, with the exceptions being the Morocco and Afghanistan areas. It will be noticed that these two areas are also the only ones which do not fit precisely into the forty-seven to forty-eight hundred mile radius. The little known Morocco phenomenon, if plotted exactly, would actually be found to be covering most of Algeria, and the Afghanistan Triangle, plotted precisely, would be found in northwestern India and Tibet. The reported effects of both of these areas are to be found northwest of their geometric centers, and I am assuming the reason for this is the fact that each area is located over a land mass, thus causing some sort of a shift.

No doubt the greater notoriety of the Bermuda Triangle and the Devil's Sea comes from the fact that they are located in some of the most heavily traveled waterways in the world. It would seem the phenomenon we study is akin to a crapshoot, and the heaviest traveled areas of the known ten Triangles would

naturally generate the greatest number of sevens, bec
dice are thrown in these areas than in the others.
from what can be learned from the available evidenc
unnamed force is in operation in all ten areas.

Semantically, there also seems to be unconscious c
in the very language used to name these areas. The term
Bermuda Triangle is actually a misnomer, because when the
known disappearances or other strange events are carefully
plotted on a map they cannot fit into the triangle drawn from
Miami to Bermuda to Puerto Rico to Miami. In terms of the
events the triangle is actually a near circle or lozenge shape. The
language which does us this disservice though turns around and
describes beautifully the relationship of all ten areas to each
other. Lines drawn from each Triangle center to the others in
all possible directions yields ten not quite equilateral triangles.
They spread out across the equator and span the globe east and
west, slightly north and south of the Tropics of Cancer and
Capricorn.

These are facts which will become more pertinent as the
discussion continues, but, for the moment, the above information illustrates the first of many perceptual problems
encountered when drawing on a two-dimensional map and
attempting to show three-dimensional realities. Unlike those in
the time of Christopher Columbus, we know without doubt
that the world is nearly round. We know it is round because we
have been told by those who should know, and we have seen
reason to trust their word. The evidence to make us agree with
them is a common model of the world, a globe, and
photographs from space further convince us of this absolute
reality. In the time of Columbus it required a thought experiment, backed by few accepted facts, to visualize the world as
round. For a person of the fifteenth century, it required an act
of faith to accept the notion of a round earth. For us to examine
the Bermuda Triangle anomalies in our time requires a similar
type of thought experiment, and, when confronting the facts,
a similar act of faith.

Using a globe, it will be noticed that if a thin rod were pushed
through any one Triangle point the rod would emerge in a
straight line in the opposite hemisphere at an opposing Triangle
point. For instance, a rod pushed through at the Bermuda

Triangle would emerge off the west coast of Australia, and the rod would become a pole between these two mystery areas. Experimentally, I have been geometrically forming Triangles along both Tropics and across the equator, but by doing so I am left with a world neither a sphere nor a pyramid of triangles. In this model it seems as if something is missing, and the missing something is to be found at the axis points of the earth. Measuring across a globe it is seen that the north axis of the planet is the same distance from the Bermuda Triangle as the Triangle area is from its nearest neighbors. The same is true at the South Pole. By recognizing the North and South Poles, and by driving our rod between those two additional points, we have a comprehensive illustration of a geometric solid called an icosahedron or, because these points are being plotted on a sphere, an icosahedral. Derived from the Greek, the name icosahedron refers to an object with twelve points and twenty sides made up of nearly equilateral triangles. When these twelve points are plotted on the spherical body of the planet Earth, each point represents a reported area of strangeness which contradicts our twentieth century viewpoint of the world. If people of the fifteenth century would have regarded our accepted idea of the world as being a little hard to swallow, what accepted knowledge of the twenty-first or twenty-second century might we regard as being unbelievable?

The North and South Poles of our planet are not without their own tales of strangeness. Some of the more common stories about the Bermuda Triangle involve UFOs, and in this there is a link with the poles, for they, too, abound in sightings of flying saucers. But other stories about the polar areas which are not necessarily associated with the Bermuda Triangle mysteries provide a key clue about the nature of the other ten points in the earth icosahedral system.

Some of the irregularities reported about the poles, especially about the North Pole, involve the migration of bears, caribou, musk ox, and other birds, animals, and insects to the north as winter approaches. Some explorers have said that above eighty degrees latitude the weather seems to get warmer, and the closer one approaches the North Pole the warmer it becomes. A tale is even told of a ship which attempted to sail to the North Pole

8

and was driven back by a dust storm. In the very far north large areas of colored snow have been examined, and the strange coloration was found to be caused by vast amounts of pollen evidently blown in by a north wind. When the Eskimos were first asked where they came from they pointed north and related the story of ancestors arriving by large birds. Far to the north or south, magnetic compasses are useless just as compasses are sometimes of little value in the Devil's Sea or the Bermuda Triangle where true north and magnetic north are the same. United States Navy Rear Admiral Richard E. Byrd, after his 1947 flight over the North Pole spoke almost mystically of the ". . . land beyond the Pole. That area beyond the Pole is the center of the great unknown." This was just one of Admiral Byrd's enigmatic statements. To this day the public has been told little more than the fact of Byrd's flight and not much else. The reason for this I will leave for others to speculate about, but a quick look at a map shows there is no land where Admiral Byrd spoke of land. Intercepted radio messages relayed to us and reported in the newspapers of the time told of green mountains and a large mammoth type animal crashing through the brush beneath Byrd's plane. But again, the map we are familiar with shows only sea and ice under the supposed position of the airplane and no place for brush to grow through which a mammoth might crash.

Some writers have gone so far as to take these and other bits of evidence and to construct a theory which states that the world is hollow. It is supposed to be equipped with a central sun to provide heat and illumination for the inhabitants who fly out of fourteen hundred mile wide holes at the poles in their flying saucers to make sure all of us untrustworthy outer-worlders aren't about to blow everything to smithereens with atom bombs.

The evidence for this kind of theory is impressive. After all, how could the Great Ice Barrier be formed up there if not by a river running from the warm inside to the cold outside? Certainly the ice pack is made of fresh water floating in salt water, and to add to this problem sometimes gravel and rocks are found in icebergs far to the north where there is not supposed to be any land. There are a lot of problems with the hollow Earth

9

theory which was formulated for the most part before satellites began taking long range pictures of Earth, but chief among the defects is the attempt to explain factual aberrations of nature on a purely physical level. It seems we can still regard our planet as being solid, reasonably round, with no gaping holes at the poles, but what about all the evidence to the contrary? What about polar bears running north to get warm in the winter? And what about Rear Admiral Byrd? What the heck happened to him?

Briefly, Admiral Byrd loaded up his plane with gas at a point as close to the North Pole as he could locate a fuel dump, then flew the plane grid north, straight at the axis of the planet. He ostensibly flew over the North Pole some seventeen hundred miles, turned around, and retraced his route back to the base. In 1956 the Navy and Admiral Byrd did the same thing in the Antarctic, flying some twenty-three hundred miles beyond the South Pole. In the words of Admiral Byrd, "The present expedition has opened up a vast new territory." Byrd referred to the land beyond the South Pole as, " . . . that enchanted continent in the sky, land of everlasting mystery!" Strange statements indeed to describe what should have been a twenty-three hundred mile vista of ice and snow.

Let us examine what might have happened from a platform of terribly oversimplified physics. As we reckon the passage of time the planet revolves around its axis once every twenty-four hours. Therefore we can say of a person standing on the equator that he is traveling in reference to an arbitrarily fixed point in space at one thousand miles per hour, since the planet is nearly twenty-four thousand miles in circumference at the equator. It is realistic to say, then, that another person standing at the Tropic of Cancer is not traveling as fast relative to the same spacially fixed point, and, to complete this mental experiment, a person standing one foot away from the North Pole axis is only one short step away from the other side of the Earth, but, rather than taking that step, if he chooses to ride the planet around to the opposite point in space he will have to wait twelve hours for the planet to revolve halfway around its axis. Our man at the North Pole, in a straight line, is two feet from his opposite point, but by waiting for the Earth to carry him there it will take twelve hours to travel the three feet in a half circle at the agonizingly slow velocity of six feet per day or three inches per hour. But the fellow at the equator, being some eight thousand miles in a straight line from his opposite point in space, will traverse twelve thousand miles at the rate of twenty-four thousand miles per day, or one thousand miles per hour. Both of these people are traveling at the same rate of one revolution per day, but one is moving 63,357 times farther than the other, yet they are both riding the same body.

This simplistic mental experiment provides a crude glimpse into Einstein's theory of relativity wherein he stated that space is curved. But more to our point it shows that without any doubt at all Admiral Byrd's airplane physically exceeded the speed of the planet below him long before he ever reached the pole. As a consequence it may very well be that Byrd never even got close to the actual axis of the planet, but veered off into somewhere and even, perhaps, somewhen else. There is a vague analogy here to my fly buzzing around inside the moving car, but Admiral Byrd's plane had no windshield in front of it to explain the effect. The ground below the plane was physically slowing even as the plane maintained a constant rate of speed. This effect is similar to the fly being able to leave the protection of the car, yet holding the car's effect, thus magnifying the fly's normal rate of speed to fifty miles per hour. One of the thought experiments which brought Albert Einstein to his well-known conclusions was the wondering of not how soon will the train get to the station, but how soon will the station get to the train.

It may be that an airplane traveling above the equator at, say, two thousand miles per hour is violating the speed limit of the local space about it, and as a consequence arrives at its destination a little bit late, but not so much as to be noticed. Einstein told us about clocks running slower at the rim of spinning disks than clocks at the axis, and we all know the astronauts are a second or two younger then the rest of us purely as a result of the relativity of speed and the lack of gravity. I do not know the speed of Admiral Byrd's plane, but even if it was only a paltry hundred and fifty miles per hour at the point where the Earth's relative velocity about its axis reached a hundred and fifty, the ratio between ground and plane speed would be climbing with every foot traveled beyond that point. If Byrd in fact flew over the physical axis of the Earth the ratio between ground speed and air speed would have been about one hundred and fifty to one. By comparison our two thousand miles per hour jet over the equator is creeping, and from the safe vantage of our relative static position at home we might be inclined to measure Byrd's movement across the North Pole at near escape velocity. Even though the people in the airplane would always consider themselves traveling at a constant rate, a witness at the equator, should he be able to measure the speed differences, would swear the plane was going some twenty-three thousand five hundred miles per hour.

This is only one way to look at what may have occurred. Actually, the twenty-three thousand five hundred miles per hour speed is simply a convenient juggling of numbers. Most of us have heard of the relativistic effect of time dilation while traveling close to the speed of light. The effect gets worse the closer to light speed one gets, but Byrd was traveling across a space that was narrowing. Perhaps the faster he went from our point of view, the further he had to go from his. Theoretically, at infinity, the exact middle of a spinning disk does not move at all, so Admiral Byrd and his crew were flying into the eye of a huge vortex and, seen from this standpoint, the only way Byrd could have crossed the actual North Pole would have been to reach the speed of light.

The Earth as a spinning body is creating or is a vortex whirl which all of us are caught up in and traveling with, and the gravitational pull of the planet is the windshield which allows us to duplicate the fly's trick and not be thrown into outer space. Admiral Byrd violated the natural motion of this vortex which we all recognize as our reality and cut across it, in essence straightening out his and our part of curved space. He came back to us by simply retracing his route and thereby reversing the effect. For the moment I am on as shaky ground as the hollow Earth people, but knowing where Byrd was going may help solve part of the Bermuda Triangle riddle.

All of us are familiar with many types of vortex whirls. A tornado, water going down the drain in the bathtub, the motion of the solar system, and the galaxy itself are all vortex whirls. Each one exists inside the other, cutting across the larger and leaving its effects. But are there unseen vortex whirls that can suck up ships and planes like soap suds going down the drain? And if there are, what are they and how can they be used or avoided, and what is their purpose in the grand scheme of things?

There are several known yet unseen vortex whirls about the planet, and some are charted on air routes as places to avoid. The most well-known one is just outside the small town of Gold Hill, Oregon. Called a gravity vortex where trees grow leaning north, pendulums refuse to swing east-west, and changes in mass are suspected, the vortex is measured at 165.375 feet in diameter with a 27.5625 foot buffer zone called a corona separating one reality from another. Animals refuse to enter this strange, small area, and its magnetic effects extend thousands of feet above, giving fits to aircraft instruments.

What causes this relatively harmless abnormality is not known, but its effects have been so well documented that should we suspect the Bermuda Triangle to be another form of vortex whirl, then a study of the Gold Hill anomaly as a known entity can shed light on the nature of the other, more dangerous vortex whirls located at the icosahedron points in the planetary icosahedral system. As a model the Gold Hill phenomenon can tell us a great deal.

The most important aspect of the Gold Hill vortex is the realization of the existence of the corona, that twenty-seven foot protective zone melding two separate realities into one. Exactly one-sixth the diameter of the vortex itself the corona encircles the entire vortex area like a thin donut, seemingly holding the vortex in and keeping the normal world out. As the rest of the evidence is examined the importance of the corona will become more apparent.

More pieces to the puzzle are gleaned from other sources, from four separate, seemingly unrelated pieces of evidence one of which is well-known and which may help explain more of the quandary. In examining these next examples it is important for the reader not to question each part on its own merit, but to wait until the information has been melded into one package before rendering judgment. It is also not important to implicitly believe that any of these events actually occurred. As in any study, scientific or otherwise, we must act as though what we suspect to be truth is the truth until it has been proven not to be. To do otherwise would mean we could never ascertain the apparent real truth, and we run the risk of closing our minds against a new truth.

There is a much published story of a midwestern farmer disappearing into thin air in front of his wife, children, and the family doctor. Forget the possibility that this incident, allegedly occurring in the nineteenth century, might never have really happened, but believe for the sake of argument that the incident really did happen.

Next accept as real the improbable story of a private pilot experiencing a near midair collision with an old pre-World War I flying machine in the skies of Ohio in the early 1960s. According to this story the modern airplane's wing tip actually touched the other machine before losing sight of it in the clouds. The tale goes on to say that the old airplane was found months later under a pile of rotten hay in a barn being torn down, and that the old plane's pilot's log told of an encounter with a large, silver flying machine which nearly killed the pilot. The date of entry was about 1911.

Next accept as truth the story of a man listed as a missing person in the New York City police records of the late nineteenth century who suddenly appeared on Broadway of that same city in the early 1950s. Allegedly the experience spooked the man so badly he panicked, ran into the street, and was killed by a passing car. Much has been written about strange disappearances, but little information regarding strange appearances ever seems to get into print. What is known or suspected about unexplained appearances can greatly add to the overall picture.

Incident number four is the best known story of all. What can the 1945 mission of Flight 19 tell us, and what can this well-publicized mystery have in common with the disappearance of a man walking in his horse pasture, the appearance of a man on the busy streets of New York, and the weird encounter of two men and machines separated by fifty years?

Perhaps too much has already been written about the

disappearance of Flight 19, and from publishing to publishing the quotes of more than thirty years ago have changed so that the precise evidence has no doubt been lost. Still, the existence of the mystery vanishing of Flight 19 is a fact, and the documented data is clear enough to provide a linking of clues for solving a major portion of the entire Bermuda Triangle mystery.

In fitting these clues into the puzzle there are three provable facts from which to work:

1. Flight 19 did, in fact, disappear without a physical trace.
2. The Gold Hill gravity vortex and its effects do exist.
3. The recent proof of what used to be known in theoretical physics as the Schwarzschild radius, is now a fact as popularized in the concept of black holes.

From attainable measurements of the Gold Hill vortex we know that a vortex affecting mass and gravity has a corona exactly one-sixth the diameter of the vortex proper. We also know this corona area is part of the world as we know it, and, paradoxically, part of a world we do not know, or part of a world known but changed. Therefore there exists two separate lines of demarcation. One through which we cross into the corona where we can still communicate with our familiar world, and one where we cross into the vortex where we cannot experience exactly the familiar world. In the case of the Gold Hill vortex the effects are not quite this bad, but the vortex created by a rotating black hole is this extreme.

Until recently we understood a black hole as a giant star so compactly collapsed in on itself that a spoonful of its matter weighed thousands of tons. So dense and heavy is the material of a black hole that this spoonful would sink in a slab of concrete like a rock sinks in water. Now this understanding has been enlarged by realizing the black hole is not just sitting still in space capturing everything near it with its immense gravity field, but it is, in fact, rotating about its own axis just like any other celestial body. So dense is the black hole that nothing can escape its gravitational pull once past the line of demarcation where the pull reaches and passes the Einstein number into what we regard as infinity or the speed of light. Even light itself is hopelessly swallowed up by the black hole, unable to escape past this line of demarcation called an event horizon, even at more than 186,000 miles per second.

In the literature there is now a rather solid theory which states that a spaceship capable of matching the speed of revolution of a black hole can use this mysterious body to plunge through a corridor to emerge an instant later several light years distant. Thus a spaceship pilot attaining orbit about a black hole at some four hundred million miles per hour will actually see a corridor in space nearly seven hundred yards across into which he can steer, and once through this narrow hole he will have been transported instantaneously many light years away from his starting point. Shades of science fiction, but there is now a beginning place for actually finding the science fiction writer's hyperspace which he has his characters use to cross immense distances of space in a very short time. And remember, I am still dealing with accepted theoretical fact! My own theory has yet to be fully explored.

With the black hole knowledge, coupled with the Gold Hill data, we can examine Flight 19 in a more revealing light.

We know Flight 19 was in contact with others for several minutes prior to vanishing completely. During those few minutes the crew members of the five single engine Avenger airplanes were disoriented. The sea looked strange. Instruments were evidently useless. The sun was of no help in ascertaining direction. Five pilots and experienced navigators were utterly lost in broad daylight in reasonably good weather on a familiar course. This in itself is a situation one might think to be impossible.

To pull some of the pieces together let us suppose Flight 19 crossed the first line of demarcation and entered the corona of an as yet unidentified and dense vortex whirl. Still in the normal world, but not quite, yet still able to communicate via radio. An analogy here could be the spaceship in orbit around a black hole. Aimlessly flying about in this limbo, Flight 19 crossed the second line of demarcation and was no longer in this limbo, but also no longer in our normal, familiar world. From our point of view they vanished. This is the fact from our standpoint, but a question of much greater significance is to find out what happened from Flight 19's point of view.

When entering the Gold Hill vortex it can be theoretically stated that one loses about ten percent of his weight or mass, but this cannot be practically proven. If a two hundred pound man weighs himself outside the vortex he cannot then take himself and the scale into the vortex and expect the scale to read one hundred and eighty pounds. The man and the scale both change inside the vortex. The scale is subject to the same laws of relativity as the man and will continue to dutifully read two hundred pounds.

The men and machines of Flight 19 were all composed of solid matter, and science tells us that matter cannot be destroyed, only altered. Flight 19 cannot have vanished into nothingness but had to conform to the universally accepted laws of relativity. Flight 19, then, went on in reality, but obviously not our reality. Where, then, did they go?

It is not enough to say they fell into the fourth, fifth, sixth, or any dimension, the reality of which we cannot recognize or logically number, or to say they dropped through a time warp. We do not know what a time warp is, even if the language is properly describing such a thing.

My hypothesis assumes they encountered some sort of an unidentified vortex whirl, and if we achieve some small understanding of where they went, we may be able to recognize what type of vortex they entered. In laying the ground work for this theory I assume the existence of at least two unknown types of vortex whirls by their strange effects upon our comfortable, familiar, normal world. I mean the unknown vortex whirls of the North and South Pole regions, and the unknown vortices located at near equal distances from each other and the poles. One of these unknown vortices is located within the area called the Bermuda Triangle. A third type, which is used as a model, is the relatively static and permanently located gravity vortex at Gold Hill in southwestern Oregon.

The vortex at Gold Hill is measurable and fixed at one geographic location, and so are the two much larger vortices the effects of which are encountered near the axes of the spinning planet. However, the Bermuda phenomenon seems only fixed within a certain rather large area, but never fixed at a precise and constant longitude and latitude. A crude analogy can be made to the drain in a bathtub, but with the drain never being found at the same spot at the bottom of the tub. We must find out why the things which happen in the Bermuda Triangle seem to be selective. Why does just one plane or boat go down the drain when others a few miles away remain untouched?

One can always return to a predicable, precise point to find the Gold Hill vortex, and one can always navigate across the face of the globe to find the Earth's axis, but if one searches for the center of the whirl in the Bermuda Triangle area he would always be involved in a new search covering hundreds of square miles of ocean. Gold Hill is fixed on the map, and so far as the poles are concerned the globe is the map. Consider another thought experiment: A hypothetical person is at a fixed point in space above the North Pole. Because of the Earth's axis tilt of some twenty-three degrees of arc relative to this arbitrarily fixed point, the axis of the planet would describe a crazy sort of circle upon the map of our dweller in space. If the globe itself could not be seen by this mythical person we have sat up in space, he could only pin the effects of our North Pole into a large circle or lozenge shape upon the face of his space map as the pin point of the axis traced upon it.

This mental experiment provides a possible correlation between the poles and any one of the ten Triangle areas referred to earlier. To expand the hypothesis, this correlation suggests the moving vortex within the Bermuda Triangle may somehow be the result of an unseen planet, of a type we do not know, wobbling on its axis with its orbit, perhaps being the circumference of our planet. The circle of disappearances within the Triangle area may be the moving bathtub drain with the surface of the Earth being the bottom of the bathtub.

This proposed explanation, apart from sounding a little crazy and being a bit simplistic, describes a very complex set of universes acting upon one another in an unseen manner. Unfortunately, there is very little in the language that can be used to discuss this supposed phenomenon. Like others, I can talk about parallel universes, time warps, and other dimensions, but these things are not part of our observable everyday world, so I must deal with the emerging evidence in simplistic, crazy sounding metaphorical terms.

blem with describing something which cannot
ured involves not only the lack of descriptive
eory of relativity. In fact, it can be said that it is
ativity. As shown by Albert Einstein, there is
____ point anywhere in the universe from which to view any
given event. Two different observers cannot see and report in
exactly the same way an observation of any single event.
Therefore we must strive to understand the mystery in terms
with which we are familiar. In this sense the very telling of my
tale is a truly colossal anisotropic grappling with an intangible,
though real, problem.

For instance, when I say the vortex at the North Pole is
tremendously large, the vortex in the Bermuda Triangle is very
small, and the Gold Hill vortex very tiny, I am defining a
problem from our local point of view. Should we be standing on
a planet which is somehow creating our Bermuda Triangle,
then our Bermuda Triangle would be, from our new point of
view, tremendously large. Simplistically, and for the sake of
agreeable description, I will say the Bermuda Triangle is the
entryway to A microcosm, and the North Pole is the entryway
to A macrocosm. To keep the arguments always in an understandable language with recognizable terms we must always
remember these are descriptions of indescribable events and
things from our local point of reference. If this is not kept firmly
in mind, then the things being described will have no validity in
the mind because of a tendency to think I am speaking of real
three-dimensional things in the familiar world.

Presented so far is data which arbitrarily makes our real,
round earth into an unseen geometric icosahedron with twenty
triangular sides and twelve points, each point the apex of a
single five-sided pyramid. The tour guide at the Gold Hill
vortex speaks of the Great Pyramid of Egypt as having been
built right in the middle of a similar vortex, but those who have
experimented with the relatively new science of pyramidology
might tell us the physical presence of the pyramid itself causes
the vortex. Those who have built models of the Cheops
Pyramid claim all sorts of phenomena including razor blades
being kept sharp and the dehydration of organic matter kept
inside. But one common reaction of all models of the Great

Pyramid at Giza is that of radiesthesia. Radiesthesia is the conscious movement of an implement such as a wire, pendulum, or the forked stick of a water dowser when held in the hands of a human operator. If a pyramid model is aligned with its flat bases squared with the magnetic poles of the earth, rods will cross above the pyramid, and dowsers' forked sticks will react. If the points of the base of the pyramid are aligned north-south there is no effect, but while in this position the placing of a bar magnet in the pyramid, with the poles pointing to any two opposing flat sides, will cause the radiesthesia effect to return.

A pair of coat hanger wires bent straight, with a handle bent at a ninety degree angle for the hands, will suffice to prove the effect. The wires are held straight out from the body, one in each hand and parallel to each other, and, most generally, when the operator walks up to the model from a north-south direction the rods will cross exactly over the apex of the pyramid. When one approaches from the east or west the rods will open up and actually turn all the way around, hitting the operator on each of the upper arms. The one exception to these effects seems to be when the wires are held by a left-handed person. With a left-handed person the effects are sometimes reversed, crossing at the east-west approach and opening at the north-south approach.

As a part of the theory it is also very instructive to notice the easy manner in which scale models of the Cheops Pyramid can be made. To be in exact scale the angle from the ground to the apex must be at an inclination of fifty-one degrees, fifty-one minutes of arc. To achieve this one need only draw a circle of any size on a flat piece of cardboard and then divide the circumference of the circle at five equal points. Lines are then drawn straight from each point on the circumference to the center, and to each other so that one is left with a pentagon outside shape embodying five triangles inside. The next step is to cut out one of the triangles and pull the remaining four triangles together to form a four-sided, three-dimensional pyramid.

An interesting correlation to the theory lies in this four-five relationship. A four-sided pyramid will cause a dowser's rods to move, but a five-sided pyramid will not. However, the geometric shape of the icosahedron with twelve, five-sided pyramids will cause the rods to move. Generally, when the rods are placed above an icosahedron, the rod in the right hand moves above the model, and the rod held in the left hand moves away to hit the operator's arm. By placing a bar magnet inside the model with the poles vertical, the rods will cross when approaching from any direction.

Clearly, something outside our current understanding happens when these simple geometric shapes come in proper alignment with a magnetic field, and it appears to be more than a coincidence that our own planet, as seen through the presented data of strange areas, conforms to an icosahedral shape. Obviously, though, our planet is not a solid, angular shape with points sticking out and a polyhedron of triangular sides. Also, we learn by taking the radiesthesia rods to a sphere that no reaction is present with or without a magnet near. This seems, to the skeptic, to end my argument, but the clincher comes by putting a sphere in motion spinning about an axis. Above the axis of a spinning sphere the rods will duplicate the same effects as above a stationary icosahedron, and the way in which the rods react changes by tilting the rotating orb, thus altering the spacial location of the rods to the sphere.

It has long been a scientific curiosity as to why a baseball curves in midair. In fact, if the baseball is a balanced sphere it should be impossible for it to curve, but anyone who has ever stood at home plate with a bat in his hands facing an expert knows just how possible it is. Perhaps, when whatever causes the radiesthesia effect is discovered, the answer to the paradox of why a baseball curves in flight will be provided.

But what does all this have to do with a disappearing farmer, an appearing New Yorker, planes from different eras nearly colliding, and planes dropping completely out of existence in the infamous Bermuda Triangle? Answers are found in the black hole theory, the theory of relativity, and, specifically, at the lines of demarcation of a vortex whirl.

Part of the original Schwarzschild radius theory, which led to the discovery of black holes, stated that at a given point, if one person of a twosome fell into the radius, or black hole, each would have a different experience which could not be communicated to the other. To the observer outside the radius, the person who fell in would not seem to go anywhere at all, but the person who fell in would indeed experience a fall in a finite period of time to the center of the gravity field, and neither of the two would be able to communicate with the other by any means, because the line of demarcation would be receding at the speed of light. Schwarzschild himself was dealing with a legitimate thought experiment, but, the fact is, neither party would be aware of the other's status. To say this is to say simply that each party simply disappeared from the other.

Science has given us the term event horizon rather than line of demarcation, because the black hole itself cannot be seen, much less measured, to provide spacial coordinates of the precise point of departure. The term event horizon is a perfect description of a line of invisibility, but I will use the term line of demarcation when referring to the Bermuda Triangle phenomenon, because this terminology better describes the relationship model of the Gold Hill gravity vortex. Bear in mind, though, that event horizon is also an apt description when looking deeply into the things which happen in the Bermuda Triangle.

The key question to ask here is what happens at the precise point of disappearance. What occurs, and what are the options of the person hovering right on the line of demarcation?

In one of my examples the farmer in his horse pasture was observed walking back to the fence to greet the family doctor when he winked out of existence. This was the experience of four onlookers, but what was the farmer's experience? At the precise point of demarcation the farmer's familiar world probably vanished, perhaps at that point, to be replaced by another world. By the same token, the strolling New Yorker found his own world dissolving, but he seems to have reacted to this similar experience differently than the farmer.

From the farmer's point of view, his world disappeared or was grotesquely distorted, and if we assume his focus at that moment was on his wife and children, his immediate concern was probably for them. They vanished from his sight just as he vanished from theirs. He rushed forward, calling their names, in an effort to stop whatever was happening to them, and in so doing crossed the last line of demarcation, sealing his own fate. The New Yorker, upon entering this same kind of wayward vortex, may have done an immediate about face and rushed away from the craziness confronting him, but he had already put one foot into an alien world. His rush back was against a current approaching infinity, and, as with anyone who gets too close to a black hole, time had slowed.

There is one report in the Flight 19 literature which claims someone heard a radio transmission consisting only of the planes' call letters some two hours after the planes must have run out of fuel. By the same token, the farmer's children claim to have heard their father's voice calling to them a month after his disappearance. If we visualize the nose of one of the planes in Flight 19 already across the line of demarcation, with its tail still within the corona, then we can surmise the radio signal, traveling at the speed of light, was battling its way out of a Schwarzschild radius effect and therefore delayed several hours. In terms of distance in our normal, everyday world the signal would have had to originate out near the perimeter of the solar system. The voice of the farmer took nearly a month at the speed of sound to reach out and be heard. A month is about the time it would take for sound to travel from the moon if it were possible. As for the New Yorker, walking from here to the moon and back would take several years. A few seconds in finite time to him, but at twenty miles a day, about sixty years to us.

Perhaps this line of demarcation or event horizon can be stretched like a rubber band allowing two worlds to be viewed at once, as in the case of the near collision of the planes from different times. The uses to which these vortices could be put, or what their various effects are, have yet to be fully explored, but some interesting speculations can be made. One such speculation involves the reported sightings of ghost ships in the Bermuda Triangle and other places. Remembering Schwarzschild's thought experiment, we see that the person who did not fall into the radius cannot see the actual plight of his companion, but instead sees him eternally at the line of demarcation. What he sees is really a light image left imposed on the event horizon. Under the right conditions are ghost ships the holographic image of the ship the moment it crossed over?

In our space shots, which rely on the proper trajectory to get from here to there in space, we must wait for "windows" to open up in the sky. Are there other kinds of windows which travelers might use to their advantage?

The one event common to both the poles and Triangle areas about the globe are the frequent sightings of UFOs. Most of us are aware of the great distances to other stars, and, as seen from the present state of our technology, the stars will always be too far away for us to reach. For this reason, many believe that UFOs cannot be visiting the earth from planets about other stars. But suppose the science fiction writers are correct? Suppose there is a way to capsulate distance? The black hole theory now allows one possible way in which to travel vast distances in an instant. Light year jumps, in fact. Science fiction writers have long fallen back on the notion of hyperspace to allow their characters to visit all the stars they wish. The very popular starship *Enterprise* of the "Star Trek" television series used a warp drive to travel faster than the speed of light. Science has its particle tachyon which supposedly travels faster than light, and Einstein was heard speaking of particles which pass through solids as having gone through the fifth dimension.

What about the science fiction writers' thesis of hyperspace? Certainly if a hyper, or other kind of space, exists it must belong to someone else; remembering relativity, the space we occupy must then be someone else's hyperspace.

Consider very carefully the above paragraph, for hidden in it is a clue of truly immense importance. If our normal space is somebody else's hyperspace, then our hyperspace is somebody else's normal space. This science fiction notion of hyperspace should not be confused with the idea of superspace put forth by Professor John Wheeler of Princeton University. Professor Wheeler has made it respectable to speak seriously of other universes, and his interpretation of quantum mechanics theorizes a superspace which acts as a doorway, or window, to multiple universes. My borrowing of the idea of hyperspace assumes hyperspace to be any one or all of Doctor Wheeler's multiple universes, not merely the doorway.

In order to make visual the emerging theory it is necessary to draw diagrams which, unfortunately, are no more properly representative of actual truth than is a word analogy. Such diagrams embody the terrible problem of showing in two dimensions drawings depicting a three-dimensional model, of a fourth-dimensional possibility, of a fifth-dimensional reality probability. Unless such diagrams depict a use to which the unseen, suspected reality can be put, the diagrams would not only be practically useless, but almost impossible to draw. In describing these effects, the reader is once again asked to keep in mind relativity, for I must speak of things not known in our terms, using the only devise available to me with which to communicate, our language. Also, the language must describe things of other worlds in terms of things from our world. An analogy would be a preacher attempting to tell the flock of a way of life and the things to be found in heaven. This is a practical impossibility because the one is not the other, not to mention that the describer has not visited the place about which he is talking.

So, again, I say in advance that the concept which I am about to discuss further is not representative of absolute truth, but rather the depiction of a truism. As stated before, I am painfully aware of the communication problems involved and know I am speaking scientifically in metaphor.

With these preliminary discussions done and the evidence assembled, I will now attempt to pull the selective and, admittedly, arbitrarily chosen evidence into one comprehensive picture. I realize the evidence reflects the picture, and the picture reflects the evidence, but somewhere between these mirrors the image of truth is peeking through like a cherry, hidden by leaves, just waiting to be plucked.

CHAPTER THREE

Fitting the Pieces

I HAVE STATED THAT the Bermuda Triangle is not alone in the world. I have shown that there are, in fact, ten such areas, and that these areas are almost exactly the same distance from each other. I have stated that both the North and South Poles are also subject to mystery, and that the poles, seen in relation to the so-called Triangle zones, form a geometric shape called an icosahedron. An icosahedron is one of two known angular geometric shapes which cause or react to radiesthesia when aligned properly with a magnetic field. I have demonstrated that the same effects of radiesthesia happen with a spheroid shape as happen with an icosahedron at rest, but only when the sphere is set to rotating about an axis.

I have shown that measurements taken from the Gold Hill vortex, an existing, known gravity vortex, can be used as a model to describe the shape and action of suspected vortices located off the coast of Florida, at other places about the world, and at the poles of the planet Earth.

My theory claims the Bermuda Triangle to be a window to a microcosm, and the poles windows to a macrocosm. In other words, something disappearing in the Bermuda Triangle can be said to have gone *down* the drain of this vortex, while something which might disappear at the North Pole can be said to have gone *up* the drain of this, relatively speaking, larger vortex.

I have shown that a vortex whirl can be many different things, and, in terms of a hypothetically fixed point in space, the planet Earth is more than a large vortex whirl of weather patterns. It also has magnetic and gravitational forces which produce whirls, or are vortex whirls which cannot be seen, but which leave effects to identify them. Understanding in our peripheral way, theoretically, at the axis of any spinning disk, wheel, or sphere, there is a point which stands still at infinity. Infinity, in this sense, might be better understood by the analogy of a person trying to get from point A to point B by traveling only half of the way at a time. No matter what finite distance is given to the space between A and B such a person exercising this halfway rule to infinity can never arrive at his destination.

Acknowledging the poles of the planet as that strange point in a spinning disk or sphere where reality becomes different, I have asked what causes the suspected vortex at the Bermuda Triangle area since nothing can be seen to spin. My answer to this puzzle is that the vortex is the electromagnetic, gravitational, and, for want of better descriptive terms, cosmic or interdimensional effect of an unseen planet, and this vortex, still not properly classified, is one of the poles of this new planet existing in a reality not shared physically with our own reality. There is very little surface evidence to prove any of this, with the possible exception that at certain times the sea may display a small concavity to mark its location, though this is only a guess on my part. The only real evidence of spatial boundaries between what amounts to two separate universes is that people in moving craft vanish with absolutely no trace or clues as to their fate. The evidence is all empirical.

I have said this unseen planet wobbles on its axis in much the same manner as our own earth does, thus causing the pin point of the axis to move through a large circle or lozenge shape upon our space. This planet, which will be referred to as Planet X from now on, tilts this way and that, to produce seasons just as the earth does. This motion explains why the vortex itself cannot be pinned down to a precise point on our space, and it also helps to show why this vortex can exist side by side with very heavy physical sea and air traffic and only claim as few victims as it does. It would be possible to hunt blindly for the vortex for years inside the larger area of disappearances and never find it because of its rapid movement. Indeed, one must approach this window to Planet X far more precisely than a NASA moon shot, for even by cutting across a corner of the vortex, straying into the corona, or sideswiping the last line of demarcation, one would experience weird abnormalities yet manage to stay on our side of reality and not plunge across the line of demarcation.

Therefore, my explanation says that Flight 19 and all the other missing planes, ships, and people, once past this line of demarcation, became relative to a new and alien environment. The experience, apart from the imagined disorientation of crossing, would be akin to a pilot flying calmly across a tropical sea one moment and in the next instant looking down at the snow and ice of the arctic! I say that Flight 19 emerged through this natural interdimensional window into someone else's arctic area. How far south or north of this new planet's axis they emerged depended on the air speed of their planes and the relative ground speed of the new planet. A boat would emerge much closer to the axis than a plane. Conversely, a plane would begin its ascent up the North Pole drain at a different ground measurement from the axis of the Earth than a man on a dog sled. A crawling man could even approach the actual axis without entering the corona of this larger planet which I will now call Planet Y.

The factor of relative sizes, as we perceive them from our local point of reference, determines the measurement, in our local terms of the distances across the respective coronas. At the Bermuda Triangle the corona may be measured in yards, but the corona at the poles may be measured in hundreds, and more likely thousands, of miles. Thus it was possible for Admiral Byrd to fly straight into the teeth of the vortex and return. He never reached a final line of demarcation. Flight 19, in orbit, so to speak, of a much smaller vortex could have turned right, avoided the line and come home, but obviously they turned left. Unlike the extreme physical forces of a black hole, they could have escaped back across the line of demarcation. The trouble is they would have had to know what to do, which way to go, and they would have had to be carrying several times more fuel. On their new found world of Planet X they would have had to do what Admiral Byrd did on this world, but they would have had to go much farther than Byrd. The distance on their new world would be measured in their miles, but it still would be measured in our terms as yards or even inches.

A curious situation now comes into play. If Flight 19 was

28

going to return it could not have returned in 1945; although by staying in continuous flight and by having the knowledge and fuel needed to fly back up the drain, they might have reversed the Einsteinian time dilation effect encountered in the new universe of Planet X, but it is unlikely given the thesis of simultaneity. It would seem that once past the line of demarcation the lives of the victims appear to us on this side to accelerate drastically, although to the people involved time would pass normally. The terrible mind-wrenching paradox here is that none of this is true in an exact sense. Under the conditions being described the mind balks. There is no logical criteria by which to judge. Any number of "what if" scenarios can be written. For instance, suppose they landed on a nice flat spot on Planet X, figured out what had happened to them, altered one or two of their planes to carry the fuel from the others, and left together toward the pole, hoping there was enough gas to get to the line of demarcation and home. If they had done such a thing, then from our point of view they are still flying, and their hoped for arrival depends on how long they spent on the ground of Planet X. From their point of view the same universe they hoped to return to would now be strange and advanced by many, many years. Most probably, if they survived the new, and perhaps hostile alien environment of Planet X, they took as their own the local time, and they have all died of old age years ago by *our* time reckoning.

By rereading the scenarios again, the reader will most likely find an apparent error. The question asked is, if they lived on Planet X and died of old age years ago, why haven't they died of old age no matter what they did? Reason not only balks at such an inconsistency, it screams aloud, yet there is no other way to resolve the problem. Either they died of old age on Planet X, or they will arrive tomorrow still young men.

I am reminded in this case of the New Yorker stretching the line of demarcation of his private little vortex, and perhaps hesitating before turning around to run away. The hesitation may have caused him to lose six or seven decades of our time. From our perspective he was frozen in time, yet, simultaneously, from his perspective he only paused a moment to make a decision.

When viewing the two-dimensional drawings of these five-dimensional probability realities, as seen in the chapter four illustrations, one is reminded of a model of a molecule. A grotesque model to be sure, but in it is an order of a special kind. If we can obtain the proper data, relative measurements might even be arrived at so as to better comprehend the nature of the phenomenon.

If we assume the newly found Planet X to be a dimensional twin of the Earth, at least as far as relative sizes are concerned, we might assume that one year of their time is experienced simultaneously on Planet X in twenty-four of our hours. This assumption might be arrived at by recognizing the simple fact that the Bermuda Triangle area revolves on the Earth's surface at a fairly fixed geographical location making one revolution per day with the planet. A time scale ratio then might be something like 365.25 to one. Unhappily, the diagram shows the pole of Planet X making the revolution, and not the equator, which would make the problem of visualization easier. Planet X's sun must be set at right angles to our physical universe, but also set at a right angle to the time scale ratio. Again, the problem has to do with ascribing three-dimensional values to something which does not affect us in a conventional three-dimensional manner. Physically, the model we are forced to use cannot work. So even if the drawings depict the best possible way to understand the problem, any attempt to arrive at exact definitive ratios will be nothing more than educated guesses. I do know, though, that relatively speaking we are observing the effects of the very small and the very big, so my guesses have as much chance of being correct at this point as anyone else's.

If it is true that the microcosm Planet X experiences one of its years in one of our days, then the time scale ratio would be 365.25 to one. If Planet X has an axis tilt similar to Earth's, then from the size of the area of disappearances in the Bermuda Triangle we can possibly compute the relative size of Planet X to serve as a navigational ratio. If the roughly plotted circle comprising the Triangle area has an actual diameter of about eight hundred miles, and holding as an unknown factor the distance from surface to surface, the axis tilt of twenty-three degrees should allow us to speak of a planet with a circumference of about six thousand miles, or a working physical ratio of about four to one. It readily can be seen that a time scale of 365.25 to one, and a physical planet scale of four to one does not equate, but it is not the differences in sizes that should concern us, since we can no more prove these changes than we can prove the two hundred pound man weighs one hundred and eighty inside the Gold Hill vortex. The ratio becomes important when viewed against the distances which can be relatively covered. If Planet X is similar to Earth, and there is no reason to suppose it is not, then our instruments taken into the vortex are going to show a planet twenty-four thousand miles in circumference for the very same reason the scale inside the Gold Hill vortex still weighs the man at two hundred pounds.

To get another picture of what we are up against, the argument can be carried up the drain into the environment of the larger Planet Y. If it is proper to say the Earth is Planet Y's Bermuda Triangle, this puts us on the low end of the four to one physical scale. In terms of our measurement of time, if one of our years is but one of Planet Y's days, then our North Pole moves through all the tilts of its axis in twenty-four of their hours in the same way Planet X's pole rushes through the entire Bermuda Triangle area in one of our days. This description is not an absolute either, for there are times when the effects of the vortex seem to be fixed. But as regards the big picture the statement is a truism, and local time and space phenomena merge in a manner the finite mind finds difficult to comprehend. Those moments when the vortex seems fixed occur only to someone in motion near the vortex, and then the apparent static position is only the illusion created by the time differentials. To keep the argument above water long enough to grasp the overall meanings, I will maintain that this rapid movement is the precise fact, and by doing so it will enable us to understand that it is no small wonder we cannot pinpoint the exact location of the vortex in the Bermuda Triangle.

If we use a jet plane for another thought experiment and assign it a rate of travel of one thousand miles per hour, we can travel between Triangle points on our globe in four hours and forty-two minutes. For the purpose of the thought experiment, I will not have our jet take a great circle route to shorten the distance. Therefore, in 4.7 hours we will travel forty-seven hundred miles from Triangle point to Triangle point across the curved surface of the earth. From Planet Y's point of reference this would be an incredibly fast rate of speed, and from Planet X's point of view horribly slow, but from our local viewpoint it is a reasonable rate of speed. For the purpose of the thought experiment, we suspend all judgment of normal mathematics and mentally move this rate of speed into Planet Y's environment without following the laws of relativity. From the pilot's point of reference his speed would not change from the constant one thousand miles per hour given him, but from our local point of reference he would disappear. To understand just what is happening we must always remember the figures are only relative to here and now. Our jet plane, having crossed the last line of demarcation or event horizon, is now invisible to us, but at what rate of speed would the plane's one thousand miles per hour through Planet Y's atmosphere be measured by us if it were possible to measure it?

Once past the line of demarcation, if our jet flies to the next Triangle point on Planet Y, or another forty-seven hundred miles as the pilot measures the miles, he would do so in his terms in four hours and forty-two minutes. But in our terms it possibly could work out mathematically something like this: Considering our year has 365.25 days, or 8,766 hours, then the time scale ratio of 365.25 to one for Planet Y yields 3,201,781.5 of our hours for one of its days, divided by the relative time in flight of four hours, forty-two minutes, times the actual air speed of one thousand miles per hour, the relative speed across the surface of Planet Y, as seen from *our* point of reference, gives us a relative speed of 681,320,106.3 miles per hour. As we measure it, the speed of light is right in the neighborhood of 670 million miles per hour, so the answer to my crude mathematical problem tells us immediately why the plane and pilot disappeared to us.

Anyone unfortunate enough to fall into a black hole would disappear to an outside observer because the event horizon would be receding from the poor fellow at the speed of light. Physics tells us that anything which exceeds, or matches the speed of light, must do so at the expense of using every single molecule of its matter to achieve that velocity. Physically exceed or match the speed of light and you will become dissipated energy. From our restricted point of view, the jet plane obliterated itself, but from the pilot's point of view a semblance of reality remains. His perception has become altered because he has entered another universe where the scattered energy we *think* he has become is simply the form of matter the pilot is now experiencing. His landscape has become different, but by his standards of judgment he still exists. Science fiction writers frequently give their characters a state of mental disorientation when entering or leaving hyperspace. Consider the known disorientation of the men on Flight 19.

There is no reason to assume that Planet Y and Planet X are any different from Earth in so far as each having ten Triangle points is concerned, so the problem of what happens to our pilot, from our point of reference, becomes even more tricky. Realizing he is traveling about one of our light years for every one of his hours in flight, and giving him as his first destination one of the nearest Triangle points on Planet Y, we feel, again, from our point of view, that he has traversed a little less than five light years. If we allow him to straighten out the warp in Planet Y's normal, curved planetary surface by allowing him to navigate a great circle route, which is the logical way to travel across a map which is curved, we can deduce a distance traveled of slightly less than four and a half light years. The four to one ratio mentioned earlier, and which confused us when placed against the larger time scale ratio, now becomes meaningful. It seems that one of Planet Y's forty-seven hundred mile trips from point to point equals a little more than four of our light years.

Almost embarrassingly, an astronomical fact nudges us, competing for recognition in our more comfortable, known universe. Our nearest star neighbor, catalogued as Alpha or Proxima Centauri, is about 4.3 light years distant.

The mathematics used for this demonstration can, and most probably will, come under an exacting critical scrutiny. The statements made in the last few paragraphs can logically be disproved by attacking the problem from a different point of reference. One can disprove certain mathematical computations, and any abstract point of view, simply by refusing to grant validity to another point of reference.

I am reminded in this case of the old story of three people checking into a hotel, each being charged ten dollars for their rooms, and then having the desk clerk realize he had overcharged each person. Calling over the bellhop, he handed him five one dollar bills and told him to make a refund to the people upstairs in their rooms. On the way up in the elevator, the poor bellhop grappled with the insurmountable problem of equally dividing five ones into three, but in a moment of selfish inspiration he solved the dilemma by pocketing two dollars and giving each guest back a dollar. The three guests now have paid nine dollars each for their rooms, and three times nine, any grade schooler knows, is twenty-seven. The mathematics goes wrong when the bellhop's pilfered two dollars is added back into the equation. Two added to twenty-seven is twenty-nine, and we know there was originally thirty dollars spent. To find the missing dollar we must take a different mathematical viewpoint. The hotel collected twenty-five dollars, the bellhop stole two dollars, and the three guests each received one dollar. Twenty-five, plus two, plus one, plus one, plus one, equals thirty.

I am also reminded of an argument between myself and a college physics teacher whereby I was trying to make what I thought was a valid point. As the argument went round and round the teacher kept shoving certain calculus equations under my nose as if they were holy script. The equations, you see, disproved my stand, but I could not convince the staunchly correct teacher that those were the very same equations that launched the revelation which I was trying in vain to discuss with him. The strongest point of view held, and I lost the debate, not necessarily because I was absolutely proven wrong, but because I had the least seniority.

My writing about the Bermuda Triangle phenomenon in this manner will cause some to peer down from lofty heights of hard found, acquired knowledge and righteously accuse me of trying to negate Einstein's universe which, I totally agree, has been proven to be correct. Equations will be trotted out, and the finger of finality will be stabbed at them. An upstart will be put in his place, and a crank will be disposed of. I wonder how much success I will have convincing the establishment viewpoint that without Einstein this book could not have been written? I wonder if the establishment viewpoint will realize that I agree with them when they show me the equation making faster than light travel impossible? In his theory Albert Einstein did not rule out faster than light speeds. He simply ruled out the ability to physically move faster than light in this universe.

The physics teacher I spoke about earlier was so busy defending a point of view contained in the theory of relativity, that it never occurred to him that I was agreeing with him. But worse, it never once crossed his mind that the very taking of an immovable stance violates the theory of relativity itself. He did not know that he was attempting to do something which his precious theory of relativity demands he could not do. The theory of relativity basically states that there is no static point of reference anywhere in the universe. In the debate I was trying to speak about a very real paradox in nature, and the teacher by not allowing the existence of the other point of view was exercising a contradiction in terms.

One of the first accusations which will be generated will be the question of what happens if the plane is only going five hundred miles per hour. The accusing finger will happily point out, when using my questionable math, that the plane is now traveling less than half the speed of light from our viewpoint. How then can it disappear from our sight? Interestingly enough, the answer may be that it can't; more probably, since Planet Y itself obviously cannot be seen, we can assume that a relatively stationary, or static position, in Planet Y's universe is operative already at *our* speed of light, and, therefore, our mental jet plane, once across the line of demarcation, is traveling, from our point of view, at the speed of light plus 11,230,106 miles per hour, or plus one thousand, or five hundred, or whatever.

Perhaps my math is far too selective, and the interesting correlations it shows only coincidence. The point being made, however, remains valid. The point is, if my theory is valid, then one could fly a conventional jet plane from here to Proxima Centauri in a little over five hours, depending on the starting point on Earth and the geographic location of the landing field.

Another conclusion involves one of the real reasons for those UFOs seen all over the planet, especially at the poles and Triangle zones. It is one of those mirroring aspects of this theory that flying saucers are using the planet Earth in the same manner a person from Utah, on his way to California, would use the state of Nevada—as a highway! Remember, we are someone else's hyperspace.

Those elusive machines we call Unidentified Flying Objects very well may be able to move through the vacuum of space, but in order to travel light year distances they never need leave a planetary atmosphere.

There are two basic directions to go when assuming these zones of strangeness are windows to other universes. Travel between stars in our universe can be achieved by using another universe as a highway, but in order to do so we must use only the North Pole—South Pole routes. The Triangle zones cannot get us to Proxima Centauri, although it would not be proper to say we could not get there from Planet X. The problem is the terrible loss or gain of local time, and if we wish our arrival at Proxima Centauri to coincide with Earth time it is absolutely necessary to use the Planet Y route. By using Planet Y as our highway, the time problems are reversed from those in Planet X's universe. In other words, a finite period of time spent in travel from point to point in Planet Y's atmosphere would represent an instantaneous arrival at Proxima Centauri, when observed from a position on Earth. As a matter of fact, there is only one way to travel instantaneously, and that way dictates not only arrival at the same instant of departure, but a traveling backwards in time as well. If one travels a given distance without a clock being able to measure departure and arrival, then the only solution to the obvious question is that time had to run backwards, and there is no reason to suppose that time cannot go in either direction. As viewed from local Earth time, it cannot be said that our jet plane arrived before it left, but the instantaneous arrival represents distance reduced to nothing, and the only way to do this is by going backwards in time while moving forward through space.

We know from the theory of relativity that a spaceship moving through space at almost the speed of light will contract time on board so that the astronauts will experience a normal space flight to Proxima Centauri in about 4.3 years of their time, but when they return 8.6 years later the Earth would have progressed many hundreds of years. By using the windows of Planet Y to make the same flight the reverse happens. From Earth's point of reference the flight takes no time at all, but from the astronauts' point of view the flight takes several hours. Now instead of the Earth being older than the astronauts upon their return, the astronauts are older than the people they left behind. However, the effects are not nearly as bad as they would be in a physical speed of light space flight. So long as one does not make too many of these trips the time capsulation could easily be lived with.

We will see later that the Bermuda Triangle truly represents a place to avoid because it is actually better described as a "time machine," whereas Planet Y can be referred to as a "space machine." Both areas affect the time-space continuum as we experience it, but unless one wants to escape civilization as we know it, Planet Y represents the route of greatest benefit.

A hypothetical navigation problem might work something like this: Planet X, causing our Bermuda Triangle, exists in Universe A. Planet Z, also in Universe A, causes the Devil's Sea Triangle, but the distance between Planet X and Planet Z in the normal curved space of Universe A is about nine light years. A native resident of Planet X wishes to visit Planet Z. He climbs in his vehicle, points it at the appropriate pole of Planet X, crosses the line of demarcation, and enters Universe B, which is our planet Earth, and our universe. He then navigates some 9,400 miles to the Devil's Sea area, locates the swiftly moving vortex, plunges deliberately through the window, and arrives near the pole of Planet Z. From there he pilots to the geographical location desired and lands, now back in his home Universe A, but many light years away from the starting point on Planet X. Depending on his speed, the whole trip would take only a few hours from his point of view, and it would be instantaneous from the viewpoint of someone on either Planet X or Z.

However, should this pilot from Planet X desire to make a truly long light year journey, he could leave Universe A, travel across the Earth in our Universe B to our pole, enter Universe

C, travel to the next pole, enter Universe D, travel to the correct Triangle point there, go back down the drain to another planet in Universe C, from there to another Triangle point on another planet in our Universe B, to the last Triangle point, and back to the desired planet in his familiar Universe A. Using the four to one ratio, my earlier questionable math, and allowing only a one point movement per planet, he would travel four light years times four light years times four light years up the drain, and then back down the drain in corresponding jumps. Assuming the vehicle made each transition from point to point in two hours, he would be traveling a little over ten hours, plus the time needed to reach his own pole, and the location on the planet for which he was steering. The distance traveled relative to his own Universe A would be something in the neighborhood of a hundred and ten light years, and this trip, though much longer, would still be regarded as instantaneous from Planet X's viewpoint.

It is not part of my theory to prove the existence of UFOs to the skeptic, for the simple reason that there are already heaps of empirical evidence which any jury sitting in a court of law would find to be binding. If everyone applied the same rules of evidence used in court to the existence-nonexistence problem of UFOs there would be no skeptics to convince. What I am saying is that if UFOs are machines brought here from other planets in the Milky Way, or even from other galaxies, this theory explains both how they got here, and in many cases, why they are here. In most cases we are no more than just a highway, and, no doubt, most of the occupants of UFOs couldn't give a hoot less about messing in our everyday lives. This is especially so for those beings who are not in their proper universe. Stopping here to fool around with us for any length of time would rob them of time relative to their home universe.

The next chapter comprises a visual discussion of this seemingly impossible theme, but, for the moment, talking about it is still necessary. In the two-dimensional drawings, the relationships of supposed interdimensional planets can be shown in precise geometric terms, but the drawings break down immediately when there is an attempt to carry them out toward infinity. For instance, the earth can be depicted as a center circle seen from a position directly above either of the poles, and the five visible Triangle points can be precisely located. Circles can be placed at these points representing Planets X1, X2, X3, X4, X5, and attached to each of these smaller circles can be placed five more earth-sized circles, each with five more X-sized circles. For several reasons this is as far as the drawing can be precisely carried.

It is absolutely impossible to represent the phenomenon on one sheet of paper. Scientists speak of the time-space continuum and represent this notion with three-dimensional models which cannot be any more precise than my drawings, because the model is not the thing being modeled. But the model can give us a handle and help us understand what they are talking about. They tell us that space is warped, that each mass taking up space is curving space, and that time is warped or curved right along with space. The closer one is to the center of a gravity field, the slower he experiences the passing of time as opposed to where he was earlier. The continuum is one thing made up of the two things, time and space. In attempting to carry the first drawing past the geometric figure of one circle surrounded by five small circles, then five large circles each having and sharing five of their own small circles, one finds he must now surround each new earth-sized circle with six Earth circles instead of five, and it cannot be precisely done and still hold the exact angles intact. One of the reasons for this is found by examining a drawing of the phenomenon from the side view.

In order to make the side view work, the small X circles must be drawn with their poles angled from the Earth circle at thirty-six degrees from the center of the Earth circle, and that puts the point of contact slightly north of the Tropic of Cancer or south of the Tropic of Capricorn. This thirty-six degree figure is arrived at by placing the center of five circles drawn on the top view at precisely measured points around a larger circle, and it is also found by measuring from the center of the Bermuda Triangle area to the center of a globe. Thirty-six degrees is also half the angle of inclination of the sides of a pentagon. Remembering the Gold Hill model of a known vortex whirl, and therefore allowing only one-sixth of the diameter of each Earth circle for its corona, the X circle fits snugly between two

Earth circles with opposing sides of its circumference against both Earth circles. A line then drawn from either or both Earth circle centers across the top or bottom circumference of the X circle to the Earth circle's equators forms an angle of fifty-one degrees, fifty-one minutes of arc.

Where have we seen this figure before, and from the point of view of my theory what does it all mean?

First, we can see by the drawings not just a navigational chart between stars, but evidence to strongly suggest the time-space continuum splits like an amoeba. The fifty-one degrees, fifty-one minutes of arc figure represents the ultimate stress point in the continuum, and when this stress point is violated time, generally speaking, seems to split from the continuum we are familiar with as a lateral movement, and space splits, generally speaking, vertically. Each split then runs into another at a right angle reforming a new continuum, which in its turn splits. If the fourth dimension is curved or warped into the time-space continuum, then it can be said that the fifth dimension is twisted. Twisted to the point where it turns itself inside out.

This idea of a time-space split is on respectable, though shaky, ground among some scientists involved in the study of quantum mechanics. J. B. Hasted of Birkbeck College, University of London, has formulated a many universe theory based on the wave function of an atomic transition. According to his theory, the wave function splits into an infinite number of universes. Coming from his point of view, Hasted does not think that spatial boundaries exist between these infinite number of universes, or at least he cannot identify them. But coming from my point of view we see not only spatial boundaries, but because of the reported surface phenomena of the Triangle areas and poles, we can locate these boundaries.

We can see the Cheops Pyramid was not angled at fifty-one degrees, fifty-one minutes of arc by accident. The angle fifty-one degrees, fifty-one minutes is now seen as the optimum movement made by Planet X in relation to its position to the two Earth planets at its poles. We can also see that the four to one ratio expressed earlier, but projected into the time split, may be more valid than we originally thought. The two ratios seem to go the wrong way, but in order for this splitting phenomena to exist at all they would have to go the "wrong way." The paradox is that an unreasonable premise is twisted back into logic or time is twisted back into space, and space twisted back into time. Time and space are parts of the same thing, and what we are looking at is a polarity switch. In school I was taught the difference between gravity and inertia, but now I'm told it is proper to think of these two things as pretty much the same thing. It is doubtful that we would know the difference if gravity and inertia switched polarity on us, any more than we can really tell the difference between negative and positive in a magnet. Both ends pick up the pin. The time-space continuum warps regardless of what we choose to call the two things which make it up.

From the drawings we can also see that the corona, one-sixth the diameter of a vortex, melding with another corona, also one-sixth of the diameter of another vortex, literally creates the X planet. But to boggle the imagination more, the Earth circle is also the creation of two coronas merging from two larger Y circles, and the Y circles are, in turn, creations of even larger coronas of even greater circles. To our poor finite minds this is an abominable fix, but through this idea infinity is served, and no matter which circle one wishes to inhabit he will always be at the exact center of all universes.

So we understand from our way of talking about it that mass warps time and space, but that another force, perhaps magnetism, twists time and space at right angles to each other. This new universe we can, if we wish, name the fifth dimension. However, once in this place just named the fifth dimension we find ourselves once again in a familiar time and space fourth-dimensional situation, so perhaps this thing named the fifth dimension should more properly be regarded as a process rather than something real and concrete.

As infinity is served by this process, so, too, is the universal concept of the One and the Many, or the generally misunderstood idea of the Trinity. The old philosophic question of the One and the Many relates to the brain buster question of why it takes two of something to make one of something else. In science, matter is broken down into molecules, and molecules are broken down into atoms. Atoms have a nucleus and an electron, and inside the atom are still more particles which are receiving scientific names such as quarks which supposedly make up the particles which make up the atom. Suspected inside quarks are still more particles ad infinitum. The best way to approach the perplexing problem of the One and the Many is by illustrating the Trinity aspect of nature. The Father, Son, Holy Ghost religious confusion seems to be a clumsy attempt to explain this two to make one concept. According to Billy Graham, the Bible tells us there is one God, but that He exists in three persons. Beyond this, the Bible and those authorities such as Mr. Graham can only scratch their heads at further attempts to explain a trinity construction which is somehow known to exist but which cannot be understood.

To make the Trinity idea understandable, I will use the analogy of a common bar magnet to show a simple trinity construction. When we speak of a magnet we refer to a whole object, the One. When we speak of the poles of a magnet we speak of parts of a whole object, the Many. To speak of a magnet as just a positive or just a negative makes no sense at all. To do so, as a matter of fact, puts one in the position of trying to defend the untenable concept of a singularity. Cut a magnet in half, and you have two magnets, each with its own positive and negative poles. Out of one magnet can come two magnets. Out of two can come four, and four can yield eight, ad infinitum. A magnet cannot exist as a magnet with only one pole, and, semantically, a magnet cannot even be sensibly talked about as simply a positive or a negative. The reality is that the seeming singularity of a magnet is made up of the duality of positive and negative. In this case, one and one makes two, two makes one, and two and one makes three. The notion of Trinity, then, is a minimum of two to any other possible number all the way to infinity, which comprises one thing.

An even more simple construction is that of a coin. A coin with only one side is inconceivable. A coin with only heads or only tails wouldn't fit into pocket or purse, and it would be an impossible singularity that wouldn't even fit into infinity.

With this in mind, the question must be asked, why five X circles near the Tropic of Cancer, and why five more near the Tropic of Capricorn? There are only two Y circles, so why are

42

there ten X circles? At first glance there seems to be a terrible imbalance. The answer is that the Earth circle can only lay claim to two X circles, just as it can only claim two Y circles at the poles. Which one of the five northern circles, and which one of the five southern circles, the Earth circle can choose may depend either on an arbitrary pick of the observer or the time of year. On a strictly numerical basis, each Earth circle in the diagram can only lay claim to two X circles because it shares its X circles with its nearest neighbors. Also, the flat diagram shows a near approach of any X to Earth happens only once a year for a duration of about seventy-three days, or one-fifth of a year, and it is this near approach which may dictate owner-ship. Also, when one looks closely at Planet Y's Universe C he finds ten Planet Ys, but even this idea of ten X or Y planets is not quite correct. As will be described later, there are really only five X planets, because the One and the Many is at work even here. One X planet is the north polarity of another X planet's south polarity. The continuum, we have seen, is twisted inside out.

If my observations are correct, disappearances in the Bermuda Triangle should be fairly heavy during a given two or three month period throughout a year. Disappearances, and any of the other phenomena, will be possible at any time of the year in any Triangle zone, but the theory tends to support more disappearances during a close approach, but involving a narrower circle inside the Triangle area. Conversely, there should be less incidents at the farthest approach of Planet X, but in a wider area. I have not plotted this idea with hard data, but if one is interested in doing so I believe he would find that more incidents occurred closer to the center of the triangle area within a certain three month time period, and that the inci-dents scattered across the rest of the calendar were further away from the center of the triangle, and at times outside the imaginary triangle itself.

In an elementary manner the pieces of the puzzle have now been assembled and fitted. No doubt pieces are still hidden, but the basic structure is now recognizable. It should be admitted at this point that this is a *re*construction. Whoever really built the Great Pyramid knew all about this, and, most probably, much more. But it should not matter what someone in the dim past knew or did not know. The only moment he had in what we regard as the past is now. The only moment we have in what we regard as the present is now. And the only moment we will ever have in what we regard as the future is also now.

The Bermuda Triangle mysteries are not solved by this theory. They are explained.

CHAPTER FOUR

The Pictorial Story

THIS SECTION IS AN attempt to make visual the many universe theory as it evolved from an investigation of the Bermuda Triangle phenomenon. Hopefully, the drawings and diagrams will benefit those who were lost or made skeptical by the discussion.

Illustration one shows the Bermuda Triangle as it is popularly recognized. The solid line of the triangle is drawn from Bermuda, to just below Puerto Rico, to Miami, Florida, and back to the island of Bermuda. But as has been pointed out by other observers, the actual area of mystery does not stay confined within the Triangle area. The dotted line gives a rough outline of the shape with which we should really be concerned. The area of mystery is much closer to being a circle than a triangle, and this observation provides a clue to understanding why the phenomenon is selective. Knowing why a ship or plane disappears while another just a few miles away goes untouched is of no small importance.

The theory states that this circle is the result of an unseen planet moving from side to side and tilting on its axis as it revolves. Thus a vortex, spatially moving within this circle, causes the incidents of disappearances and other phenomena. The vortex is never found at any static point within this circle, but ranges all over the area on the map, shown as a lozenge-shaped circle.

The actual vortex is quite small as we might measure its diameter, and a ship or plane must enter it precisely aligned toward the center in order to be swallowed. This accounts for the selective nature of the phenomenon.

Illustration two shows all ten Triangle zones as they fit on a flat world map. The Bermuda Triangle is not alone in the

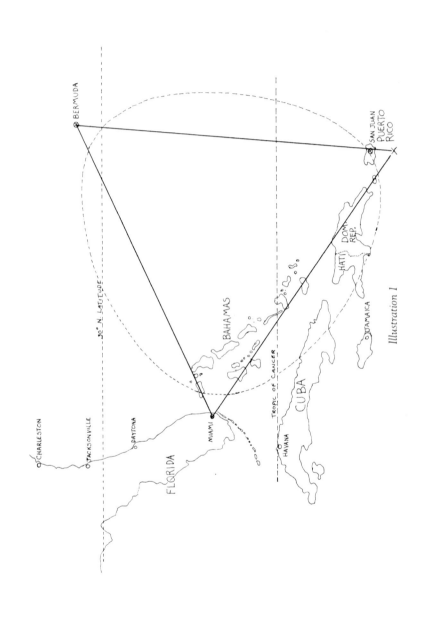

Illustration 1

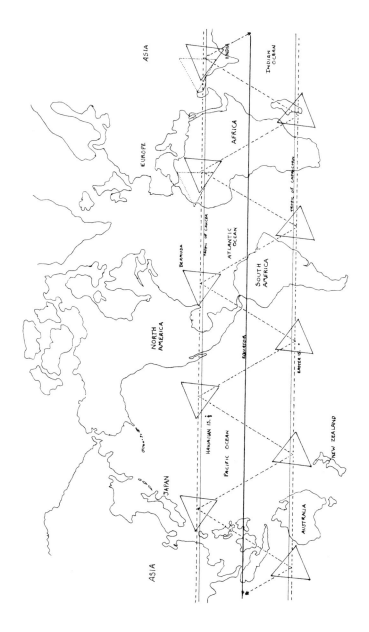

Illustration 2

Earth Icosahedral

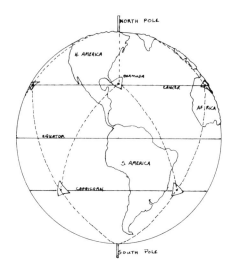

Regular Icosahedron

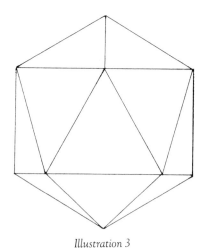

Illustration 3

world, and is not the only place on the globe where people and their vehicles fade out of reality. The other Triangles depicted here are reported to exhibit the same effects as the better known Bermuda area and the Devil's Sea, south of Japan. One notable witness of the effects of the Hawaiian area is Arthur Godfrey. He watched a military plane, which he had just missed boarding, vanish off a radar scope in this area, never to be heard from again.

Notice that the centers of the Triangles rest slightly above the Tropic of Cancer and slightly below the Tropic of Capricorn. The dotted lines connecting the centers of each Triangle area form ten larger triangles spanning the equator, and each Tropic line. If the curved surface of the Earth is taken into account, any four of these Triangles, removed from the map and formed into a three-dimensional pyramid, will give an angle of inclination from the base to the apex of fifty-one degrees, fifty-one minutes of arc—the same angle of inclination as the Cheops Pyramid at Giza.

Eight of the Triangle areas rest predominantly over water, and two of them rest over land areas. The reported Afghanistan and Morocco incidents do not lie in the geometric perfection shown by the solid line triangles, but lie northwest as shown by the dotted lines. The speculation here is that the land mass somehow shifts the actual location of the effects.

The clue in finding the location of these other Triangle areas is very important. In this diagram half of an icosahedron is found.

Illustration three shows both a regular icosahedron depicted as an angular solid and the icosahedral aspect of the planet Earth, shown by the curved dotted lines between Triangle areas.

An icosahedron is one of two known geometric shapes which, when properly aligned with a magnetic field, will react to radiesthesia when sitting at rest. A sphere will react to the radiesthesia effect in the same manner as an icosahedron, but only when it is set to rotating about an axis.

Notice that the regular icosahedron, when viewed in the flat drawing, seems to exhibit six points around its perimeter. This is an illusion on paper, but when this illusion attempts to become reality in the fifth dimension a universe split results.

49

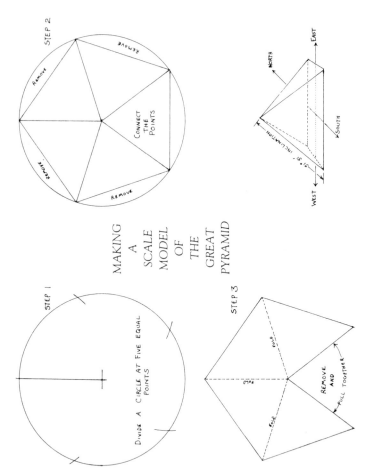

STEP 2

REMOVE

REMOVE

REMOVE

REMOVE

CONNECT THE POINTS

STEP 1

DIVIDE A CIRCLE AT FIVE EQUAL POINTS

MAKING
A
SCALE
MODEL
OF
THE
GREAT
PYRAMID

STEP 3

FOLD

FOLD

FOLD

REMOVE AND

PULL TOGETHER

NORTH

EAST

SOUTH

WEST

51° 51' INCLINATION

Illustration 4

A four-sided pyramid is the best known geometric shape which causes, among other things, a radiesthesia effect.

Illustration four shows the ease with which a scale model of the Cheops Pyramid can be made. It is not necessary to use the fifty-one degrees, fifty-one minutes of arc to achieve the radiesthesia effect, but the strongest reaction is obtained when it is used. A flatter pyramid which does not exhibit at least fifteen degrees of inclination from base to apex is practically dead, and a too tall pyramid exceeding eighty-seven degrees is also dead to the radiesthesia effect. The difference between the two extremes is thirty-six degrees, which is the precise position of an X Planet to the centers of its two Earth planets. As will be seen in illustration nine, fifty-one degrees, fifty-one minutes of arc is as far as an X Planet can move in relation to an Earth planet.

When moving out to the speed of light, the time dilation effect is not noticed until one is near the speed of light, and the closer one approaches this speed limit the greater the effect. This is also the effect produced by lowering or heightening the angle of inclination of a pyramid. The radiesthesia effect remains relatively strong until close to the fifteen degree, or eighty-seven degree points, and quickly diminishes after that.

Rather than the effects, the known and accepted measurements of the Gold Hill vortex can be used as a relationship model to describe the workings of the suspected vortex in the Bermuda Triangle.

Illustration five shows a simple construction of the vortex at Gold Hill, Oregon. Notice that the corona is precisely one-sixth the diameter of the vortex proper. When placed onto the points of a pentagon, the Earth circles will also be one-sixth the distance of their diameters apart from one another, and the merging coronas will contain the X Planet.

No other scale but the one to six ratio will yield the angle fifty-one degrees, fifty-one minutes of arc, and this seeming coincidence is difficult to dismiss.

In illustration six is seen an impossible depiction of the X Planets and the Y Planets. It has been surmised that the distance between the X Planets is a little more than four light years apart, when the distance is measured from the X Planet's point

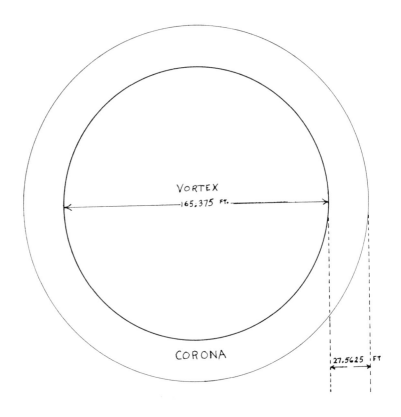

VORTEX

—165,375 FT.—

CORONA

27.5625 FT

Simple Diagram of Gold Hill Gravity Vortex

Illustration 5

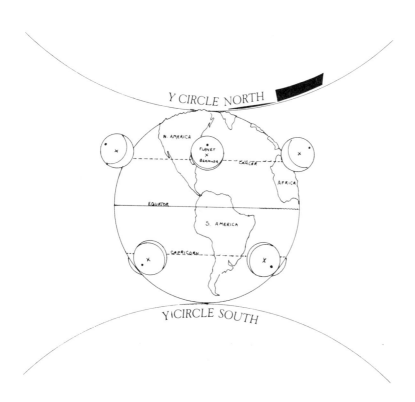

Illustration 6

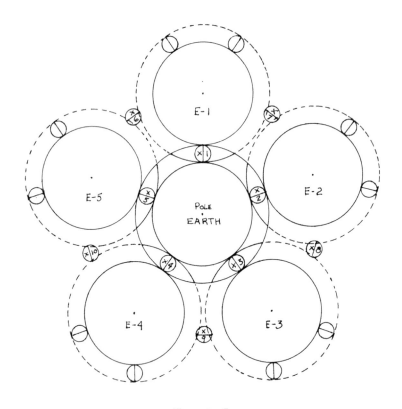

Illustration 7

of view. It has also been learned that each X Planet is at its optimum close approach only one-fifth of a year. This knowledge can account for the fact that there is only one star, not ten, in our normal space which is only 4.3 light years distant. The star in our normal space which is next closest should be about twice that distance from us, or a little over eight light years.

If we assume the Bermuda Triangle X Planet to be Proxima Centauri to the X Planet northeast of Hawaii, then the next closest X Planet from Hawaii may be the southern hemisphere counterpart of the Bermuda Triangle or the X Planet west of Australia. To seek in our normal space all ten manifestations of Earth-type planets encircling Planet Y would be folly. We must remember the Earth circle can only claim two X circles, and because of the twisted condition of the time-space continuum, only five of the ten X Planets shown are really existent. Two X Planets represent one, because each is exhibiting the opposite polarity of the other.

Illustration seven shows the molecule similarity in a top view construction. Because the diagram is flat, the X Planets six, seven, eight, nine, and ten cannot be shown touching their shared Earth circles one through five. Taking the center Earth circle as the mother planet for a constant, we must remember that the other earth circles, in a three-dimensional model, would be tilting in toward the pole of the mother Earth circle. This action would bring the circles, six through ten, back into contact with the Earth circles, one through five.

The effects of this relationship are better displayed through the side view diagrams in illustrations nine and ten. It also must be kept in mind that this drawing is only depicting a tiny slice of infinity.

Attempting to carry illustration seven out toward infinity is impossible in a flat drawing, as is shown here in illustration eight.

Notice that by trying to show the E-1 circle having five more E circles surrounding it cannot be done with any degree of precision, and that the attempt produces six E circles. This wrenching effectively produces a time and space split pushing the new planet circle into its own time and space coordinates. The drawing shows the emerging E circle (E-1-A) as being the creative effort of E-7 and E-8. Though this may not be an exact representation, it seems clear that any new planet is the product of two existing planets, so the amoeba analogy used in the text of the last chapter is not a precise representation, although it is still valid since the two circles producing one may be the north, south polarities of one circle. In some small part of the scientific ranks this function is suspected to be in the form of a wave, though it is only looked at in the microcosm world of atoms.

The top view drawings also show the time machine aspect of the many universe theory. If we use the center Earth circle as the Bermuda Triangle, then none of the surrounding E circles can be used as the Hawaiian or Morocco Triangles. In this top view drawing these other circles are exact duplicates of Earth, not belonging to our three-dimensional universe, but probably exact duplicates of our universe which we would regard

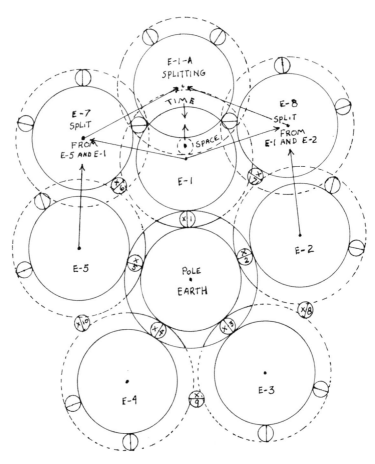

Illustration 8

as the past, or perhaps the future. Traveling to them would be possible, but meeting ourselves there most probably would not be possible, since the crossing of the X Planets to reach them would grossly distort our proper time. Should we try such a trip, it is certain that our duplicate is also attempting the same journey, so even if time were not distorted, our duplicate would not be there when we arrived, but would be on another Earth planet where another of our duplicates also was not at home for the same reason. In this paradoxical universe it is possible to envision meeting ourselves coming as we are going

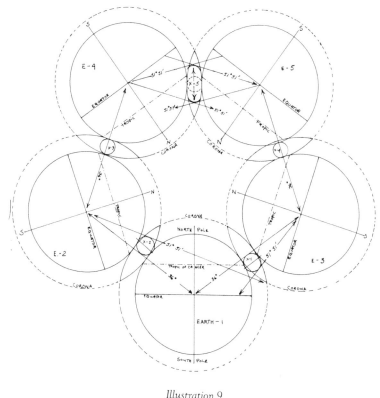

Illustration 9

across the surface of Planet X, but the two of us would have to have left our respective Earth planets in opposite directions, and this would involve a major change of mind by only one of us. Still, the possibility of meeting ourselves is left open, and it can be theoretically stated that in each of these universes, at this precise moment, I am now writing these words, and the reader is now reading them.

As will be discussed later, this condition will continue eternally, and the movement of time is more of a matter of focus rather than of physical motion. Illustration nine is the simplest way possible of depicting the many universe phenomenon from the side view.

Note that no attempt has been made to show the Tropic of Capricorn phenomenon, or to show more than one X Planet between Earth circles. The five X circles are shown in different positions within the convex areas formed by merging the Earth circle coronas. Planet X-1 is shown in its furthermost movement south of the Tropic of Cancer, and Planet X-2 is shown in its furthermost movement north of the Tropic of Cancer. Note the lines drawn from the centers of E-3 and E-2 across the bottom of X-1, and across the top of X-2. These lines represent the optimum movement possible within the convex areas. This measurement is not an arbitrary one on my part, but is taken from measuring the physical area of the Bermuda Triangle and then transposing it on the diagram. The lines of inclination were drawn in after the circle, one-sixth the size of the Earth circle, was put in. These lines, in all cases, are fifty-one degrees, fifty-one minutes of arc. Notice also that the line drawn from E-2 across the top of X-2 intersects the very edge of the convex area caused by merging the two coronas.

Circles X-3 and X-4 are shown precisely on the thirty-six degree line formed between the centers of E-2, E-4, and E-3, E-5, and circle X-5 is shown in all of its daily positions relative to E-4 and E-5. The fifty-one degree, fifty-one minute lines are again shown. The reader must bear in mind that this drawing is two-dimensional and cannot show the twist inherent in the reality, but the limits and stress points of the twisting effect are clearly seen in the fifty-one degree, fifty-one minute lines.

The side view drawing of illustration ten shows the relationship of a single X and Y Planet to the Earth. The event horizon aspect of this drawing corresponds to the point where some people think the hole is which leads to the interior of the Earth. The actual size of the event horizon area is relative and can be greater or smaller, depending on the speed at which it is approached from the Earth side. When approaching from Planet Y's side, the line of demarcation can only be found where the pole of the Earth touches somewhere within the area labeled event horizon. Notice the same thing is depicted from the X Planet's point of view, and the area of the tilt of its axis is the zone which we regard as the Bermuda Triangle. Planet Y's Bermuda Triangle is the Earth.

In the relationship of Earth to Planet Y the black hole analogy

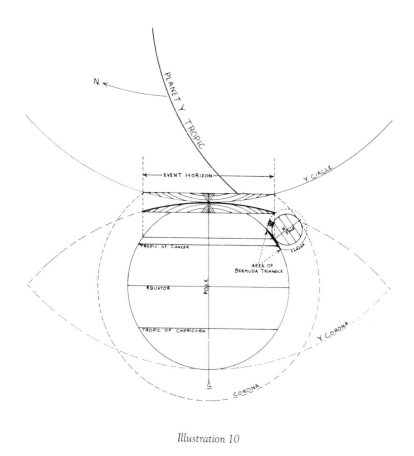

Illustration 10

cannot properly be used, because the line of demarcation is at the center of the vortex and not on the outside perimeter, but the Bermuda Triangle, created by Planet X, does exhibit the event horizon aspect of a black hole, because a true corona must be crossed and entrance is made at the perimeter of the vortex. Remember, the Earth *is* the corona of Planet Y, and to insert ourselves in the permanent environment of Planet Y requires attainment of a *relative* velocity of the speed of light.

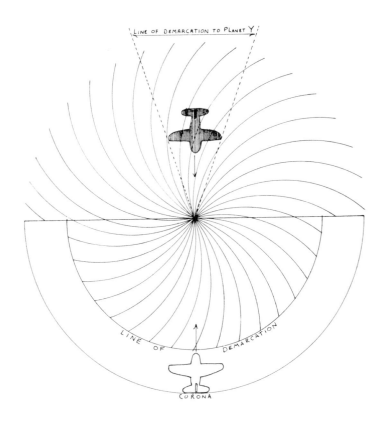

Illustration 11

The top half of illustration eleven represents a flight toward Planet Y, and the bottom half represents a flight into Planet X.

Since we are Planet Y's corona, entrance to its reality is achieved by moving directly at the axis of the Earth, or to the center of the vortex we are. The closer one approaches the axis the faster the movement would be measured from our standpoint elsewhere on Earth. At the center, where this relative speed would be regarded by Earth standards as matching infinity, the plane would emerge across the line of demarcation shown by the approaching plane in the bottom drawing.

The lower drawing shows a plane in the corona about to penetrate the line of demarcation of Planet X's vortex. When it does, it will emerge near the center of the vortex, and the distance from the center will be determined by the speed of entrance relative to Planet X's ground speed.

If either of these vortices are approached from an angle and not directly toward the eye of the vortex, the movement from one universe to another will not occur, but strange effects will be noticed. Contrary to their advertising, airlines do not cross the poles, but skirt to one side. The reason given for this is for convenience of navigation, but no matter the reason, this skirting of the poles keeps the airplanes and their passengers on the correct side of reality.

Illustration twelve is the top view of illustration four. This is also an impossible depiction, but number twelve shows us several possibilities. The drawing assumes all X Planets shown share a common universe labeled A. However, this appears to only be half a truth. If we hypothetically place ourselves on the X Planet marked Bermuda, we can exit at the pole, travel across the Earth's surface to the next closest planet, and land on another planet still in Universe A. The trip, as shown, will be about forty-seven hundred miles across the Earth, and about 4.3 light years measured with the same instruments but transposed to Universe A. The same type of trip to the planet called Z would be about 8.6 light years, and ninety-four hundred miles, respectively. However, this particular chart may not be precisely accurate, because it cannot allow for a suspected polarity balance. For instance, by taking the route shown to Planet X-1 from Planet X, we might enter X-1 at their North Pole. But if we traveled to Planet X-2 we might enter at the South Pole of the same planet. As shown, Planets X-1, X-2, and Planet Z and Z-1 may be manifestations of the same planet.

Also, from the point of view of Planet X, it probably makes little difference whether the trip is begun through the North or the South Pole, since the connection is made to an Earth planet regardless of which exit point is used. This polarity manifestation could also be the relationship between Planet X, and Planet XX, Planet Z, and ZZ. Planets X and XX may be the

Illustration 12

same planet, but in this two-dimensional drawing one has its North Pole abutted to Earth, and the other has its South Pole connected.

Rear Admiral Richard E. Byrd, in his 1947 flight over the North Pole and in his 1956 flight over the South Pole, was going to different parts of the same Planet Y.

Illustration thirteen shows a simple diagram of a long light year journey. Note that each planet circle is set at right angles to the other, and that the Tropic of Cancer and Capricorn connections are forsaken for simplicity.

Regardless of which universe is used as the highway, only

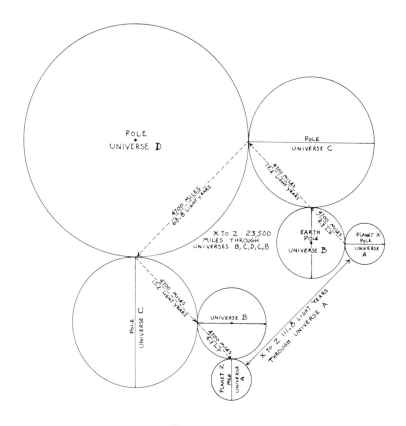

Illustration 13

forty-seven hundred miles are traveled through each circle. But as the vehicle of transport proceeds through each larger and larger circle, more and more light year movements are registered relative to distances measured from Universe A.

The diagram allows for movement of only one jump between Triangle points. Movement across Universe B takes the traveler 4.3 light years from Planet X, but movement across Universe C, in Planet X's terms, must be seen as four times that, or 17.2 light years. Movement across Universe D is also four times the distance across Universe C. As shown on paper, the inter-dimensional trip appears to take about two-thirds longer, but the mileage between Planet X and Planet Z in the normal space of Universe A is about 111.8 light years as opposed to the actual vehicle distance of about 23,500 miles. Also, the 23,500 miles and the time it takes to travel them, will only be measured by those in the vehicle. To observers on either Planet X or Planet Z, it will appear that no time was taken at all to move an immense distance.

Illustration fourteen shows what may have happened to the 19th century farmer.

In panel one the farmer sees the family doctor approaching and walks toward his wife and children, expecting to greet the doctor as he arrives in the yard. But unknown to any of them, a small, rapidly moving vortex, depicted by the dotted line, moves in his way. At this point all movement is still registered in Universe B.

In panel two he unluckily enters the corona of the vortex, and the event horizon effect obscures him from the others. But from his point of view, shown in panel three, something terrible has happened to his family, and he rushes forward to save them, inserting himself into Universe A.

In panel four he has vanished, much to the consternation of the onlookers, and the vortex continues on in its orbit across the surface of the Earth.

In panel five the farmer is forever lost to his family and becomes an unwilling resident of a new world. But if this wayward vortex represents a lunar type of environment we can be assured he didn't last long.

The farmer's children claim they heard him calling them about a month after the incident happened. This detail of the story confirms the idea of the Schwarzschild radius theory. The farmer's voice was delayed by the time dilation effects created at the line of demarcation.

Panel one of illustration fifteen has the hapless New Yorker taking a stroll to enjoy an after dinner cigar which his wife won't let him have in the house, and in the Universe B of the 1890s he approaches a wayward vortex, perhaps the same one encountered by the farmer.

Unlike the farmer, when the New Yorker realizes something is terribly wrong, he stops precisely on the line of demarcation

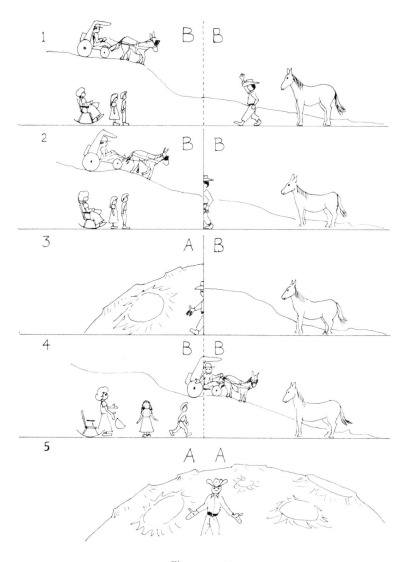

Illustration 14

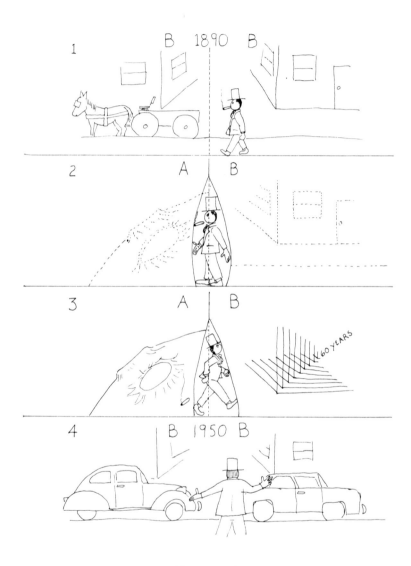

Illustration 15

rather than continuing on. Panel two depicts this pause, separating him from both Universe A and B, stretching the line of demarcation.

In panel three he turns and runs away in panic, but his entrance into the line of demarcation has separated him from the normal flow of time, and the moment spent hovering at Universe A's doorstep has caused him to lose about sixty years of Earth time, even though he has not aged a bit.

Panel four has him back in Universe B, but 1890 is sixty years away, and the panic which caused him to run away from Universe A is heightened by finding himself almost instantly transported to the alien world of Universe B, 1950. He continues his panic sprint and runs in front of an object he has never seen before – a modern automobile.

The Schwarzschild radius effect multiplied his two or three steps into a five hundred thousand mile walk and a sixty-year stroll.

Illustration sixteen, panel one shows one of the planes of Flight 19 approaching the line of demarcation between Universe B and A. At this moment the pilot is attempting to make a radio transmission, shown by the wavy line trailing behind the plane.

Panels two and three show the plane at different physical positions on the line of demarcation, and the radio signal is fighting its way out of the increasing collapse of Universe B. As with the New Yorker, this breaking out takes a long interval of finite time as it is measured in Universe B, and the signal, traveling infinitely faster than a man can walk, takes two hours or longer to be heard.

Panel four shows that once across the line of demarcation the radio signal can no longer be received in Universe B because the line of demarcation is receding at the same speed as the signal.

Panel five shows the possibility of two planes cutting diagonally across a wayward vortex and nearly hitting one another. Though we tend to see these two planes as being of different times, the truth probably is that they are of different worlds, experiencing different levels of technological

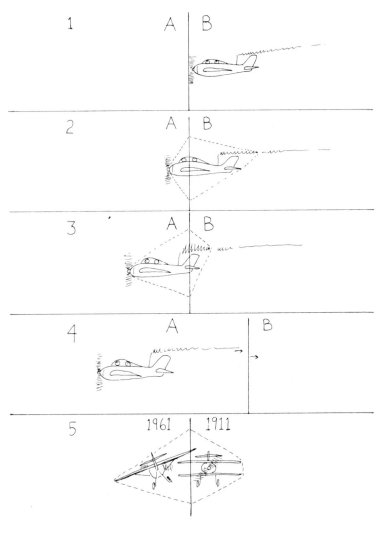

Illustration 16

development. The time separation is real in a sense, but there is no actual encroaching upon one's personal past or future.

At first glance, one might believe that with such a proliferation of vortices a person would not be safe from them anywhere, but this is not a situation which should cause alarm. Obviously, the greater portion of humanity and its machines do not disappear. The reason this is so becomes apparent when studying the whole phenomenon.

Two things must happen before one is swallowed up by a vortex, whether it is on the loose or relatively stationary. First, one must put himself in the vicinity of the vortex, and, second, he must himself be in motion. If one never visits the Bermuda Triangle area he certainly has nothing to worry about. Even in the case of a wayward vortex, if a person is fairly motionless the vortex can pass right over and not even muss the hair. In order to become the victim of an unseen vortex one also must be in motion in a direction which puts the path of approach directly at the eye. If the prime motion of the intended victim is not precisely aligned with the center of the vortex he will escape. The odds of hitting precisely something which cannot be seen are probably about the same as a blind man making a hole-in-one at the golf course.

The probability of being swallowed up by a vortex of this nature must be billions to one, and even for those who live and travel constantly in the Bermuda zone, the odds of being lost in the vortex must be several million to one given the conditions necessary for insertion through the window.

There doesn't appear to be any reason for us to run out and buy vortex insurance, but if the reader happens to be out for a stroll one day, and the world begins to fade, stop and check out where it is you seem to be going. If you don't like the looks of what lies in front, come on back. The trouble is, neither option may be any good, but once stopped on that line of demarcation there are only two choices, and neither allows you access to where you were before the whole thing got started. Should you become one of those in a billion, at least by having read this book you will be able to tell the startled people on the other side how you got into their world. Of course, should they believe in witches, you may be rendering your account from atop a pyre.

CHAPTER FIVE

Ramifications — A Look
at the Completed Puzzle

FOR THE END OF this book I had entertained the idea of including a bibliography, but such a list, in order to be complete, would have to show hundreds of books and lost articles. This short work comprises, nearly, the sum of my knowledge on this subject, gleaned from reading, listening, experimenting, and questioning, and no bibliography could possibly be complete, nor be properly representative, of a reading program for those who might be desirous of checking my sources. Such a list, though, would show a wide diversity of titles from a large spectrum of subjects. A single paragraph from one book or article sometimes correlated with two paragraphs from another book having nothing to do with the subject matter of the first, and so my reading time has been spent in enjoyment, "accidently" finding pieces of the puzzle.

Instead of a confusing bibliography I will devote the last few pages to an investigation of the consequences of my theory should it be representative of truth.

There are some noteworthy ramifications of this theory, one of which is encountered by examining the seeming contradiction of many universes co-existing in what appears to be the same place. This is where the split of time from space becomes critical, and by speaking of this I hope to render this particular argument from the contradictory, at least, back to the paradoxical.

There is an axiom that states, where there is nothing, there cannot be something, and where there is something, nothing is nonsensical.

In building this theory I wondered about the apparent splitting of time from space. How does it happen? When does it happen? Can this splitting be timed, and, if not, why not? Is the splitting fluid, or does it occur at the blink of an eye, so to speak? Universe A and Planet X do not exist to the eye, therefore, do they exist at all? Can they not exist and still be valid? The theory of relativity notwithstanding, can this other time and space, here dubbed the fifth dimension, be there in all its corporeality and still, at some point, not be in existence at all? And if this is possible, at some point in time, do we not exist?

From the macrocosm point of reference it might be said that the split happens every seventy-three days or so, but the split at the microcosm level would be so fast as to not be measurable. In fact, if what I suspect is true, there never will be a way to measure it, because there is absolutely no way to measure nothing. Perhaps the only way we can ever hope to measure this supposed phenomenon is the speed of light itself. In this case I can utilize the analogy of a movie film for real life, and use each frozen frame as it moves in front of the lens of the projector as a microscopic piece of our existence. We tend to think of light as moving very, very fast, but in a fluid, smooth motion. We also fool ourselves in a movie theatre by considering the light upon the screen to be moving smoothly, but we know intellectually that this is not true. We know the movie film consists of thousands of still pictures taken at different moments in reality, and the movement we see on the screen is an illusion created by the actual movement of the film in front of the lens. In reality, perhaps light itself plays much the same trick on us. If atoms, planets, stars, and entire universes are splitting off to duplicate themselves infinitely, might we not be *both* the frozen image *and* the moving projection?

Pick a number. Perhaps a million times a second, or half a million, or only a thousand times a second we may literally go out of existence. Intellectually, reach for this idea, but realize as you do that the very granting of validity to such a concept destroys the reality of a second. If there is such a reality as an off and on universal reality the very idea of a second, or a minute, or any segment of time becomes an absurdity. Granted that there may be a state of nonexistence, like the off cycle of a strobe light, but when the Earth is in this state of non-existence does Universe A and Planet X blink on? When our continuity invisibly disrupts here in Universe B, does Universe A experience the next frozen moment in its reality?

The theory poses questions like this that beg answers, although some will say that the answers beg questions. In the kind of universe being described, either way one looks at the problem is correct.

There is a philosophic concept which states that because you cannot be intellectually aware of something until after you have seen it, then whatever you see belongs to a past moment. In other words, there is a time lag between the sighting of an object and its cataloging by the mind; therefore, whatever is seen properly belongs to the past even as we delude ourselves into thinking of it as belonging to the present. This concept applies to everything; a dirt clod or the entire perceived universe. Everything identified by our senses belongs to the past, and, therefore, cannot be accurately regarded as real. Absolute or true reality must always be a microsecond before intellectualization takes place. The continuity of our lives, according to this concept, consists of billions of recollections like the frames of a movie film projected upon the screen of our consciousness with a minute delay from projector true reality to screen apparent reality.

Plato did not have the analogy of a movie film to use, but his idea of the essence of a thing existing before one is able to sense it is a parallel philosophy describing the same sort of idea of reality.

Should this philosophic argument be correct, then the idea of a universe blinking on and off gives a handle on where this fifth dimension might be. Should my theory be true as well, then the paradox is that the moment of non-existence, or the *off* mode, seems to be that moment we intellectually perceive to be reality, and the moment regarded to be the *on* mode is the actual reality. But in accepting these two concepts, reason demands that the real *off* mode is reality, and the real *on* blink, in reality, is the *off* blink. There is no other way to say it: Reality simply *is*, and for a lack of a better way to put it, our minds are the only reality, but we do not perceive it to be so until we have cataloged whatever is "out there" and projected it upon the screen of the *off* blink.

The only moment we can ever have to make decisions or to engage in actions is *now*. I think we can all agree on the truth of the last statement, but hidden in this simple statement is a ramification which could truly set us free should we wish to drastically alter our reality. If we look at a past object or action and mistakenly regard it as a present object or action, we forsake the actual "present" and make our decisions and carry out our actions in the past where they can have no effect on the course of our lives. Free will certainly exists, but in accepting the last few ideas it would appear that very few of us ever take true advantage of it.

Our conventional viewpoint of time is triad in nature, but this view of future, present, past does not incorporate a working knowledge of a true Trinity. The melding of future, present, past into a proper trinity construction yields a future of expected realities, a past of seen realities, and a present composed of the two realities. We cannot act out of free will from a past platform or from a future platform, but from a true present position we can act out of free will from either one. The present is the magnet, and the future and past are but different poles, alike in that they both pick up the pin and attract one another to form the One thing.

The *now* moment which we mistake as the moving phenomenon of time is all we have.

Albert Einstein gave us the abstract reality of light or the Photon particle, existing forever as one eternal second. If we are fooling ourselves about the very nature of the reality we *think* we live in, it does not take too large a step to understand the ease with which we can fool ourselves regarding the other reality which does not act upon our perceiving senses at all.

In the discussion of the Bermuda Triangle solution I pointed out that time and space seem to split from the continuum as we know it. The significance of this chases the imagination in as many directions as time and space seem to go. Reason tends to close up shop, barring an unwanted customer. Reason wants nothing to do with infinity. The faculty of logical thought cannot face infinity and still maintain a good solid hold on the world which makes up our daily lives. But in order to really take charge of our lives, infinity must not only be dealt with, it must become *known*. Reason can make a great show of explaining infinity, but it does so only to placate mind. You see, this world we consider as reality is the construction of reason and its domain. Reason is finite and certainly has an important place in the scheme of things, but mind is infinite and cares nothing about intellectually understanding that which it *is*. Reason can never *know* infinity, but somehow it must learn to trust it.

The entity of time, separated from space, means there is an infinite number of places where we exist collectively and individually. There are worlds recently split from our *now* understanding where we exist almost unchanged from our *now* consciousness, and there are worlds which split many years ago which have our duplicates in far different circumstances. A decision made on a critical issue years ago will eventually be made in reverse somewhere along the split, thus sending one of our duplicates on a different life course. And somewhere along the line one of our reversed decisions will lead to the death of one and then more of our duplicates. There are worlds where we were never born, and worlds where we died. There are worlds where Hitler won the war, and worlds where the Roman Empire stayed viable into the twentieth century. There are an infinite number of worlds the reason calls future and past, but none of these worlds were, or will be, personally ours. They all exist *now*.

This idea boggles the imagination, and reason runs for the wings, but it is not without order in the grand scheme of things. One of the more popular plots in science fiction is the time machine. All writers using this theme have constructed elaborate schemes so their characters would, or would not, violate the law of causality. The cause-effect consequence of traveling in time, as we traditionally view time, can be illustrated by the question of what would happen if one went back into time and killed one's father before one was born. The strict law of causality states that this event could not have, or has not, happened since the killing of one's own father would mean that the killer would never be born. Such an idea, were it to become reality, would close off the progress of time, everyone's time, and cause it to loop back onto itself like a snake trying to consume itself at the tail. The quite valid principle of causality prevents such a circle being closed.

On a more grand scale, what would happen if a time traveler went back to the Little Big Horn to watch Custer's last stand, but instead of just watching, interfered in some way and prevented the massacre? The law of causality states that if this could occur the time traveler would return to a present world that had no knowledge of Custer's last stand, and this same law also states that the interference cannot happen, since the present does indeed record the events of Custer's folly.

In the presence of a bona fide time machine, a Trinity understanding of time resolves the role of causality. Instead of regarding time as a linearly moving thread or current pushing us along an unwavering course from the past to the future, we should instead see time not as the past-future singularities but as the whole magnet. The magnet, of course, is the present, or the *now*.

Our irreconcilable idea of the future is never more than a vague promise, and the past, as we are personally concerned, does not exist. Such a past cannot be traveled to. The future, so far as we are personally concerned, also does not exist, and also cannot be traveled to.

There is only one moment in our lives, and that moment is *now*. Causality is a moot law describing nothing, and becomes useless as a gauge when viewing time correctly.

The present, as far as we should be concerned, is all there is, all there ever has been, and all there ever will be.

A genuine time machine can take us to a *now* moment in another separate universe with its own idea of a triad type time line, and we might, in ignorance, intellectually recognize this universe as our own past, or suppose it to be our own future, but we would be making a great mistake. We could kill our fathers or stop the massacre at the Little Big Horn, and still return to the world at the moment we left and not find one thing changed because of our actions. Our actions will affect the course of events and evoke the law of causality, but only in the *now* moment we interfered with. The place we were was not our actual past.

A good psychic can predict with a very high degree of

probability something in the near future, but the further away the calendar date is from the prediction, the lower the expectation of success. Using the many universe theory this quandary is made understandable. If we are the result of a split from what we mistakenly regard as the future, and that future is the result of a split which our future selves regard as their future, then the further away in linear time the psychic predicts, the more splits occur. Thus, the chances increase that the vision will be altered when the predicted date of the event reaches us via our contemporary notion of time.

To our senses the movement of time is a real appearing illusion. There is but one moment. If someone is asked to put a date to the creation of the universe, the only proper response is to relate the current date and hour.

The world *was* created *now*. The world *is* created *now*. The world *will be* created *now*. The past and future tense in our language is no more than a convenience to which reason has ascribed a little too much importance, and the importance assigned to the convenience nails the lid on tighter to the perceived reality.

A vague grasping of this notion of time existing as one moment can be made by one who makes the effort. It takes little mental gymnastics to accept the truth of the statement, *now*, being always correct no matter when it is stated. But what happens to space at the moment of the split?

Everything in the perceived universe must exhibit some aspect of the trinity concept expressed by the magnet and coin analogy. Nature abhors a vacuum, and science abhors a singularity. One of the agonizing problems science gave itself by finding a black hole was that a rotating black hole seems to represent a horrifying singularity. In its make up, talking about a black hole is the same thing as talking about a negative without a positive. As a scientific reality, anything, absolutely anything, can theoretically happen inside the event horizon of a black hole. Time can go backwards, a person could meet himself coming and going, and all our nice, orderly rules and laws of nature are turned inside out. As a consequence, there is a mad scurrying within scientific circles to put their own creation of the black hole back into the orderly rules of the One and the

Many. If there are black holes, and there certainly seem to be, then to balance the game out, white holes are now being searched for, both in the reality of the universe and in theory. Some of the theories being offered by respectable scientists are just as crazy sounding as the one the reader has been exposed to in this book.

In scientific theory, black holes can break out into white holes in *another universe!*

With these kinds of ideas roaming about within the very body of science, there are some respected scientists who are, more and more, being beset by a creeping worry that by so diligently looking for confirmation of theories proposed by themselves, or their colleagues, they may be actually creating the desired end product, rather than discovering something that was always "out there," just waiting to be found. This is only a creeping worry though, and for a very human reason. No sane, well-educated scientist is going to actively try to prove the creation versus discovery thesis, or even give it much serious thought. If someone managed to prove such a ridiculous notion the proof would throw this finely ordered and perfectly structured world into utter chaos. The proving of this idea would render all the careful scientific work of literally thousands of linear years into uselessness. No sane, well-adjusted person spends time, money, and effort to build a house only to tear it down.

Such a concept, proven, would mean the world, as we perceive it, is basically an illusion!

If time is an illusion, then so must be space, and the coming together of the two creates that which we regard as the reality which reacts to our senses. The melding of time and space creates the grand illusion, but we are not through being dumbfounded, or having our reason assaulted, for in accepting this idea, we must then grapple with the unsettling notion that our senses which tell us about the illusion are also illusions. It would seem that all things having to do with this world, so long as they can be named, are all illusions, but we cannot accept this idea from the point of view of the world which supplies the identifying word, illusion. By definition of the above idea, the word illusion is itself an illusion.

Such a concept of an illusory universe, proved, would affect the world at every imaginable level. For instance, would we morally condemn or congratulate the people who warn us repeatedly about the dangers of a disease such as cancer, or the dangers of eating or smoking certain things? On the one hand, they are doing a fine service by publishing their warnings, complete with graphic descriptions of the symptoms to watch out for, and on the other hand, they are doing humanity the worst possible disservice because by publishing the information they are actually *creating* the problem and showing us graphically how to contract the symptoms. An illusory world would operate on beliefs and expectations. We believe in disease, and fear is certainly a form of expectation.

I do not expect the idea of an illusory world to be proven, and, by the same token, I do expect the apparent naked singularity of the black hole to be resolved. Science will not and cannot tear down its own house. Science has unearthed an apparent singularity way out on the fringes of its own thoughts, but it has totally ignored the most far-reaching, apparent singularity of all. In this I am speaking about life. The birth, life, death triad is no more properly representative of a trinity construction than is future, present, past. Taken in its complete totality, life itself does not seem to have a balance. Speaking about life in all its melded points of view is speaking about a positive or a negative. The magnet is missing. Again, the trees are too close, obscuring the forest. That which should stand out like the proverbial sore thumb is not seen and investigated. The universe, as we perceive it, and thus life, is one grand, sweeping singularity. It is heads or it is tails, but it is not a coin.

If reality itself is blinking on and off with such a speed that no manmade shutter can ever catch the action, and if each perceived moment, projected upon the *off* screen is splitting forever outward and upward, then infinity is indeed served. But more to the point, there very well may actually be one static point of reference from which to view the universe. However, this static point does not exist within this universe (the universe we project), but exists in the reality we project from. The eternal second, epitomized by the Photon particle, is our positive side to balance the negative, and the two taken as a whole solve the problem of the apparent singularity of life.

It would appear that the state attainable by merging the two poles of our being would be a beneficial position from which to conduct the business of life, and it seems there would be only one way to experience this true or other reality. That way first involves refusing to habitually project. Stopping the world, so to speak. But once one has personally stopped his view of the world, refusing to go back to the projected *off* mode, one would experience nothing that resembles anything like his remembered life. Such a person would be like an empty vessel waiting to be filled, and, paradoxically, would appear to project from the projection. The strobe light is not a strobe light if it shines with a steady beam. The person who stopped his world would be forced to invent new situations to project from the *on* mode back to the *off* mode in order to experience anything at all. His options include nothing else, otherwise the steady beam of the *on* blink becomes another form of singularity. He may choose to return to the old and familiar world, or to sample from infinity's grab bag including a personal invention, illustrated by using the more proper word, creation.

All those who pursue one form or another of occult sciences are striving for this state, though most of them don't realize it. From the practice of transcendental meditation to witchcraft, to the ideals of so-called secret societies such as the Rosicrucians, people are blindly seeking to command the world through techniques of mind over matter, techniques of astral projection, techniques of mind reading, clairvoyance, and a host of other labels for things thought not to be of this world. Even when some success is found, reason clamps a lid on the success, hardening the illusion. Reason stubs its toe on something concrete and demands the mind accept the hard, painful reality. These techniques are empty promises, because the technique, and the name describing it, are part of the world furniture. Mind cannot move matter because reason has placed it firmly on the table and made it subject to reason's laws. Mind over matter is a misleading statement. Rather, mind *is* matter, and when seen in this light the mountain can be literally moved. The only technique that will ever work is the one that will control reason. Most generally, those who dabble in the occult have picked the wrong target. They are trying to tell the mountain to move, but it is really the reason which must get out of the way, since it is our reason which created and maintains the mountain.

In reality's *on* mode, time, space, and their continuum do not exist. Eternity is one eternal second. Time and space, and the things which fill them, are creations of the mind being created continuously. If one wishes, this process can be entered through windows to be experienced consciously on different levels. One of the more mundane of these windows we recognize by the name Bermuda Triangle.

In these pages I have outlined a reality in which anything, absolutely anything, is possible. We do not realize it, but we have already visited the interior of a black hole. We live inside one!

Should one be near a person who "stops his world" one of the effects the observer might see is the complete obliteration or disappearance of the other. The one who vanished would not have lost himself, however, but would have gained a unity with himself. He would have merged the positive-negative singularities of himself into the aware magnet of his total being and found a platform from which to launch incredible feats back into the reality he would now *know* and be totally *aware* he was *creating*. To the eyes of the uninitiated observer, such a person would be nothing short of a miracle worker, capable of any feat set out for him to do.

Seen in this light, it seems we are all the most grand of fools, chasing around in an unreal, projected world which operates exactly the way each of us individually and collectively expect it to operate. We accept the reality of the unreal, and we do not even think about the reality of the real. The only way out, we think, is death, so, obligingly, death is to be experienced even if we are enjoying the game. If one of us, or a group of us, decide to experience a concept or another reality we go ahead and do it, even if it flies in the face of another's experience. Our perceived world is a mass of seeming contradictions. The best example of these apparent contradictions is to ask which of the myriad religions in the world can be singled out as the true way. Without getting too deeply involved in the obvious controversial nature of this question, there is only one suitable answer: All of them. Here a restatement of the most grand of all paradoxes is warranted: all, absolutely all, points of view are valid!

A Christian cannot be convinced that a Moslem is correct. A Moslem cannot be convinced that a Hindu is correct. A Hindu cannot be convinced that a Buddhist is correct, and none of them can be convinced that they are all correct. But they are all correct. They have gotten together in their respective groups and *agreed* on how they wished to view reality.

Remember the Einstein quote which ended my introduction? "It is the theory which decides what we can observe." The view is the reality. For those who believe their position represents the absolute truth this idea is nothing short of the worst possible blasphemy. No doubt I would be better off cursing their gods than telling them they are all correct. For cursing their gods I could be forgiven, but for telling them they are all correct, in their viewpoint, I have attacked them on a personal level. If they dare to even listen they will have to deal with the notion that they may have spent their lives doing something which was not necessary. Tell the Christian that he has created God in his own image, and beware the wrath of the creator who thinks he has been made from a greater mold. It is easier to believe that one is right and the rest of the world wrong, than to believe that everyone, regardless of his beliefs, is right.

Jesus Christ, who probably knew all of this and more, because he had found by experience his two singularities and brought his negative and positive poles together to form the magnet of his person, told us that any two or three of us who would get together and *agree* on what we wanted, could have what we wanted. Anyone who feels comfortable seeing things this way can find several such references in the Book of Matthew, and, specifically, chapter eighteen, verse nineteen.

This world is a semantic construct. This book is semantical in its contents and in its physical being. Any book is such a semantical entity, including the Bible, and as such is subject to interpretation. Interpretation is one person's idea of another person's ideas, and in this there is a golden opportunity to miss the meaning of what was really said. Almost without exception, all branches of Christianity have misconstrued what Christ was

81

trying to tell us. You see, most of us, in this case, chose to comprehend his reported words from a point of reference different from that from which he was speaking. Christ must cringe every time a preacher ascends the pulpit to tell the flock what he thinks the Bible says, and Buddha must throw up his hands in despair whenever a Buddhist priest informs the faithful of the meaning of his words. In fact, they both must have felt somewhat chained by trying to communicate a concept that words cannot convey, and the demonstrations meant to help the explanations were transmuted by the faithful into petty miracles. What must really rankle, though, is that Christians have screwed up Christ's words in "His name."

As far as this book is concerned, I know some will screw up the meaning of my words, and I can hardly wait to see what I have said when my ideas come from a different mouth.

Understanding reality from the point of view of a many universe theory can do one of two things to the individual. It can clear up the mystery and point to a path which will lead one to find his totality where he will be able to operate with any view of any world, *knowing* exactly what he is doing, and thus be "blest," or this understanding will clash too harshly with the perceived reality, driving the person even more solidly into the singularity of this reason constructed reality. In this case he is "truly cursed." At the very least, acceptance of this idea of a multifaceted reality can, with a certain finality, answer the age old question which caused all these religions to spring up in the first place: Where will we go when we die? Wherever we want to go.

There is only one time, and that time opens up into any space we wish. A word of warning is needed here regarding these words. The sort of statement just made can fire up the fervor of those who believe in reincarnation, but before the statement can be misunderstood in this fashion, I need to say that the concept of reincarnation is just as valid as any other belief. So don't get too fired up, and if you really don't want to get involved in the cause-effect dogmatic idea of Karma, you needn't bother. It's really not necessary.

Perhaps the reason so few of us are able to truly follow and emulate people like Christ, Buddha, Mohammed, Lao-Tzu, Confucius, and many others, is that by doing so the mystery of life is no longer a mystery. And we do love a mystery.

I, myself, had a love affair with the Bermuda Triangle mystery, but once having arrived at an answer, at least an answer suitable to me, I now have the knowledge that those who read my conclusions will not be as intrigued as I was. You see, if the reader of this book agrees with me, then the reader no longer has the mental chewing gum of the mystery to mull over. A solved mystery is no fun at all.

The physics teacher with whom I argued could not possibly accept my point of view. Deep down he wanted to solve the "riddle of the universe" himself.

The answer to the Bermuda Triangle mystery as explored in my theory is a simplistic look at a complicated, though logical, process, and if someone such as a theoretical physicist with all his degrees and credit cards wishes to investigate, I can tell him there are plenty of mysteries yet to be solved. If he can accept the basic principle of this book, there still is all the room in infinity for him to complicate the process still further. There is an eternity of mysteries available to him, so long as he forgets that he created them in the first place.

For the engineer and technician, I leave the mystery of how to use the Bermuda Triangle for the "benefit of mankind."

For the parapsychologists, I can only tell them to put away their testing apparatus. If we live in a universe where anything is possible, what's the point of working so hard to prove the existence of something which their own existence proves? Anyway, they will never prove physically the existence of something which isn't physical; all they can possibly do is observe the effects of a momentary Trinity frame of mind. They should reach, instead, for their totality.

To the solidly religious I can only shrug my shoulders. If they are comfortable believing the rest of the world wrong, then they are right. If they think I am deluded, then they are still right, but I think they are deluded, so we are both right, and if they don't care to agree with that, then I don't care. It's their delusion, and I hope they enjoy theirs as much as I enjoy mine.

I'm sorry, but I can't resist getting in the last dig, twisting the knife just a little bit in the back of all our personal and collective delusions.

If the mystery is fooling ourselves, then the solution is fooling ourselves twice.